I0141394

Tablets for an Unavoidable Victory

Pastor Elvis DAGBA

Elvis Dagba Ministries

Copyright © 2017 by Elvis Dagba Ministries, LLC. All right reserved.

Published by Elvis Dagba Ministries, LLC
P. O BOX 9733, Norfolk, VA 23505

No parts of this book may be reproduced, stored in a retrieval system, or transmitted in any form or by any means, electronic, mechanical, photocopying, recording or otherwise without prioer written permission of the publisher except as provided by United States of America copyright law.

Scripture quotations are from the King James Version of the Bible.

ISBN-13: 978-0998442808
ISBN-10: 0998442801

First Edition

Printed in the United States of America

CONTENTS

Acknowledgments

This book is dedicated to all divine creatures that have the breath of life within.

All honor and glory to God our Father, who in his infinite grace has permitted the writing and editing of this work. His fidelity, his love, and his all-powerful will finish in us, this work that he began. Everything is for Him, because of Him and through Him. Amen!

During his ministry, Pastor Elvis Dagba saw the recurring problems that people face. It was by seeking God's response to deliver souls that God, in His grace and great love, spoke to Him. The Holy Spirit revealed the origin and causes of many of these problems to his servant.

By reading this book you will undoubtedly find common ground with your lives and of those around you. It will be like a light on the hidden works of darkness. He will also give you the answer and allow you to enter a new dimension of freedom and grace acquired through the death and resurrection of Jesus's love.

Good reading under the guidance of the Holy Spirit.

Pastor Elvis Dagba

CHAPTER 1

YOU ARE YOUR NAME AND YOUR NAME IS YOU

We cannot get into the thick of things without having given in advance the definition of the word "NAME".

Definition: The word **"name"** is used to refer to a person, an animal or thing, then distinguish things of same species. The name expresses a title, a qualification and we can say that without the name, nothing can be identified and no one can be either.

Knowing the name of a person allows us to know his character *(Being)*. It is for this reason that the angel of the Lord asked Jacob: "what is your name?" and he answered: "My name is Jacob" (Genesis 32: 27). This kind of question has been asked several times in the Bible; Moses also asked GOD by saying "but if they ask me what your name is, what shall I tell them?" (Exodus 3: 13 and 14). God replied to Moses by saying: "I am the one who I am supposed to be". He added: "so you shall say to the children of Israel, he who is called "I am" has sent me to you". It means: "I can do anything, I am the Almighty; there is nobody else above me. When I say yes nobody can say no."

The name carries a great mystery; in this way, the name you carry can be both a source of blessings as well as a source of curses. Your name has a meaning to it, even GOD's name has different meanings. For instance,

JEHOVAH RAPHA: GOD who heals; JEHOVAH SHALOM: GOD who gives peace; JEHOVAH JIREH: GOD who satisfies the needs. There is a force or a spirit under any name. The Holy Spirit supports excellent names and evil spirits cling to the common names to destroy the carriers of these names. By reading this book you must have more clarification of the name you carry. Is it supported by the Holy Spirit? Or the evil spirit? Be illuminated in the name of Jesus Christ of Nazareth!

What is the role of the spirit bound to each name?

The spirit attached to each name reveals the characters in that name and the promises that are attached to one hand, and leads to the achievement of the intention or the desire of the donor on the other hand. Let's consider the case of Abraham and Sarah; they have become carriers of these names because God wanted them to be fertile.

What is impossible with their previous names that were Abram and Sarai? This couple has drained sterility throughout their life until their old age and God decided to fulfill his plan in their life, hence it appeared necessary that their name should change:

Abraham = High Father, Father of Nations
Sarah = Princess (Genesis 17: 5-6 and 15-16)

God can also do this for you, if you give yourself to him and if you put your faith into action. A new name will bring new and positive testimonies upon your life. All for

God's purposes and accomplishments in your life. Even your enemies will be forced to call you by your new name. As long as you say "Yes" to your name, if it is a good or positive name then you will be blessed, but if it is frivolous or trivial name you are cursed. The tragedy is that every day you answer at least once "yes" to your name. Ask yourself the question what is the explanation that is bound with your name and to whom you answer?

We have seen people change their names in this life after becoming aware of the curse against them because of their name and GOD has made a change in their lives. Yes! GOD can give you a new name that the sorcerers, fetishes and marabous are obligated to call you by that name.

Example: GOD gives you the name **Prosper**. Someone asks a fetish priest to make you become poor. Before the fetish priest pronounces incantations on you to make you poor, first he calls your name *(the spirit of prosperity that is behind your name will respond)*, the fetish priest will say, Prosper, I order you to become poor and the spirit of prosperity will say "No! GOD declared him prosperous and it will be so forever, Hallelujah!"

A man of God after following such instruction visited his village to learn about the real meaning of his first name, that was APEDO. He knew from the information obtained that APEDO means "empty House or ruined house". During a war, all his ancestors were dead, but her great grandmother who survived with pregnancy. She gave birth to a boy and gave him the name of APEDO. She said,

"You will be called APEDO because you were born in an empty house destroyed by war." Since then, the offspring carries that name until now.

This servant of God thought and said then "Can an empty house get married? Can she make achievements? Can she evolve? Then he decided to change APEDO into Elijah *(Prophet of fire)* since then, his life took a positive turn.

This is to tell you that carrying a cursed name curses you and doesn't exclude any social class. Either you take the way of deliverance or you change your name completely. Let me tell you, a bad name brings desolation and an excellent name gives you prosperity. The name and the holder are closely related, they form an inseparable even a closed entity. You are like your name; you cannot carry a good name and not be blessed, this is not possible. The character of a person reflects his/her name.

<u>Some examples of negative and vulgar names followed by their impact in the life of the holders:</u>

KOUWE N'DJINAN *(Born to die or born for death)* in Fon tongue; such a man was a brilliant student, on the eve of his hiring, the death broke.

KOUGBLENOU *(death has devastated)* in Fon tongue. This is a whole family that carries this last name, and all members of this family are still dying at the age of 40.

MEDAHEVI *(son of poverty)* in EWE tongue

The richest in this family has a BBCT moped and no member of the family could purchase their own house.

There is a brother called KOMBO in Lingala tongue, the name means sheep. The life of this brother is always going from failure to failure. He dreams and sees himself in a closed cage while eating grass. As soon as he was informed about the meaning of his name, a work has been done and GOD brought glory in his life. Before that he was always dependent.

Do not take anything lightly. Even the names of neighborhoods, cities, companies, and public places influence these places.

Example: Cross of Death: blood still flowing at this cross place *(fatal accidents)*.

In a country in the sub-region, some parents consult the timetable for naming their children while others refer to fetishes or worship of the family (OUSSOU-ALLANGBADJE), names from rivers or stream (COMOE-BENDAMON), names from trees (ALLA, KPANGUI), names born of stones (YOBOUET), from the hill or mountain, (OKA) or others names like KANGAH *(slave),* NAFISSOU *(uncertainty).*

There are also in the Bible negative names as:

Nabal: foolish man (1 Samuel 25: 25)

Jabez: suffering (1 Chronicles 4: 9-10)

Ichabod: without glory (1 Samuel 4: 21)

Remember that iron sharpens iron, in this way, the name influence the neighborhood and relationships. Are you under the negative influence of your name? Maybe the problem you are experiencing originates from the name you bear. You need to be delivered. Come to us; and we will help you get out definitively from negative effect of your name.

CHAPTER 2

SCHEDULE OF 120 NAMES AND THEIR MEANINGS

Numbers	Names	Meanings
01	Abel	Breath/Vanity
02	Abraham	Father of Multitude
03	Achan	Trouble
04	Adeline	Kind
05	Adolph	Wolf
06	Albert	Firm
07	Alex	Aid
08	Alexander	People defender
09	Alfred	Peace prosecutor
10	Alphonse	Noble
11	Alphonsine	Noble
12	Ambroise	Alive
13	Amelie	Pain/Suffering
15	Amos	Bearer of burden
16	Anne	Grace/Favor
17	Antoine	Powerful in faith
18	Anthony	Strength
19	Ariel	Lion of God
20	Aristarchus	Good governor
21	Arthur	New
22	Augustus	Venerable
23	Bartholomew	Son of Talmai
24	Basile	King
25	Benjamin	Son of easiness
26	Bernard	Courageous
27	Blaise	Sweetness
28	Blandine	Tender

Numbers	Names	Meanings
29	Bob	Famous
30	Brigitte	High
31	Camille	Sacrificer
32	Caroline	Strong/Power
33	Celine	Conceal
34	Cesar	Courageous/Chief
35	Chantal	Who sings
36	Charles	Strong/Free
37	Christian	Who is with Christ
38	Christopher	Who carries Christ
39	Claude	Affectionate
40	Claudin	Lame
41	Clement	Benevolent
42	Constant	Faithful
43	Cornelius	Intense Desire
44	Cyril	Heavenly
45	Daniel	God is my judge
46	David	Beloved
47	Deborah	Bee/Hard working
48	Denis	Treasure
49	Diane	Goddess of the moon
50	Dominique	Master
51	Edward	To Keep
52	Ernest	Serious
53	Elvira	Guardian
54	Esther	Star
55	Eugenia	Well Born
56	Fabian	Kindness
57	Felix	Happy/Joy
58	Firmin	Solid
59	Frank	Courage
60	Frederick	Peaceful
61	Fulbert	Shiny
62	Gaelle	Generous

Numbers	Names	Meanings
63	Gaspar	Peace provider
64	Gaston	Host
65	Gedeon	Valiant
66	Georgette	Glory
67	Guillaume	Protection
68	Hagar	Fleeing
69	Helen	Light
70	Henry	Leader
71	Hilaire	Joy/Glee
72	Ida	Obscure/Hiding
73	Ignace	Powerful
74	Jeremy	God gives
75	Job	The Persecute
76	Jocelyne	Joy
77	John	God give Grace
78	Jorge	Fortunate
79	Joseph	Who adds
80	Josaphat *(Jehoshaphat)*	God is Judge
81	Judith	Praise
82	Julie	Sweet
83	Lazarus	God rescued
84	Leah	Tired
85	Lot	Veil
86	Luis	Better
87	Lydia	Clear thought
88	Mark	Defender of Men
89	Matthew	Gift of God
90	Mireille	Like Mary
91	Monique	Only advisor
92	Nadine	Hope
93	Nadia	Light
94	Narcisse	Numbness
95	Nicholas	Victory
96	Oliver	Anointed

Numbers	Names	Meanings
97	Odette	Wealth
98	Pascal	Warrior
99	Paul	Small
100	Peter	Rock
101	Philomena	Goodness
102	Placide	Who loves calm
103	Regina	Queen
104	Robert	Bright/Shiny
105	Rodrigue	King
106	Roland	Earth
107	Romeo	Intelligent
108	Rose	Farmer
109	Rudolph	Handsome/Charming
110	Samson	Small Sun
111	Sebastian	Honored
112	Severin	Demanding
113	Sophia	Wisdom
114	Stephen	Crown
115	Sonya	Wisdom
116	Sylvie	Forest
117	Terry	Gift
118	Urielle	Light of God
119	Urbain	Courteous
120	Victor	Winner

Beloved, you are just like your name. Maybe your name is not mentioned in this chart. You must try to get information to get its meaning and get the deliverance if necessary *(if your name bears a curse behind)*. The list is very long; if you cannot find the explanation for your name, then come to us and we will inform you. If your name is a burden to you then change it; or if you need deliverance from your name, we can help you because God did not change the names of everyone in the Bible. For instance, Jabez has always kept his name but he broke the influence that is bound to it which means suffering. May God be glorified!

CHAPTER 3

THE WATER MERMAID AND HER EFFECTS IN FAMILIES

Definition: **Mermaid** - The Mermaid can be defined as a fabulous being, with a woman head and upper body and the hindquarters of a Fish. The mermaid job is to attract people.

Origin of the Mermaid

Ezekiel 28: 14-17: "you were a guardian cherub protector, with unrolled wings; I have placed you and you were on the holy mountain of God; you walked among the glittering stones. You have been integrated in your ways since the day that you were created, till the one when the iniquity was found in you; by the greatness of your trade you were filled with violence and you committed the sin. I will send you away from God Mountain and I destroyed you; you, covering cherub from glittering stones. Your heart was lifted up because of beauty, you have corrupted your wisdom by your brightness and throw you to the ground, and I will send you to the Kings for their use."

The mermaid is an agent of the devil. Satan, the fallen angel hurled to earth, he formed his government. This government in which the mermaid has an important role as the Prime Minister of the satanic government. Ninety nine percent of the problems humans are facing are caused by this spirit.

Field of Action

Revelation 12: 12 "that's why rejoice yourself, Heavens and all of you who live in the heavens. Woe to the earth and the sea, because the devil has rushed down to unto you, endowed with great anger, knowing that his time is little."

Two places are mentioned in this passage; the earth and the sea.

John 10:10 "the thief comes only to steal, kill and destroy; but I have come so that the sheep may have life and be in abundance." The Bible tells us that the devil has three missions name: stealing, killing and destroying.

In its fields of action which are the earth and the sea, this spirit operates together with two demons that are called night husband and wife.

How does this spirit possesses the bodies?

1. The worshiping of water by ourselves and/or our parents.
2. The fetish way to find a husband or wife.
3. The search for healing from a witch doctor or marabout.

4. Attendance at nightclubs. Night clubs are a favorite place of the spirits of night husband and wife. He who goes then to night clubs is in constant contact with these spirits (*especially as it is the center of debauchery and immorality in all forms who settled there*).
5. The affection of pornographic films.
6. The invocation of spirits to have children.
7. Sexual intercourse with a person that possesses the spirit (*sexually transmitted*).
8. The wearing foot shackles.

Indices (*obvious signs of possession by the spirit*)

- Mysterious disappearance of personal belongings (*money included*).
- Playing with snake in dream, seeing it in a dream also.
- Swimming in a dream.
- Physical Fear of water.
- Imagination of the presence of the snake around.
- Feeling the smell of perfume or fish around.
- Narcissism leading to spend his time candling.
- Sexual intercourses in dream.
- Inability to maintain a lasting relationship with the opposite sex.
- Hate of marriage.
- Kidney pain, lower abdomen and genitals pains; (*demons are using the sex of animals to hold intercourse with the human dream, reason of the presence of these evils*).
- Quarrel with the partner after sexual intercourses (*disgust with the partner after the sexual intercourses*).
- Getting married, having children or being pregnant in a

dream.

- Premature ejaculation.

- Have a weird ease of finding money with several partners.

The real purpose of this spirit is to maintain its dominance over your life and to have the right to harass you, manipulate you, plunder and tear you. In one word to destroy all good things that are for you. His intention is to make your life a bin or a pile of garbage, so you will hardly spend your life without a husband and with sicknesses. **Isaiah 4:1 "and seven women shall take this day one man and will say, we will eat our bread and we will wear our own clothes. Let us only bear your name! Take out our shame!**

His work in families and his strategies

The family is a group of people composed of the father, the mother and the children in the strict sense of the term; in the broad sense of the term, the family consists of a set of people with a parental relationship.

After further study, it was revealed that 75% of families in the world are owned by the spirit and his objectives are division, separation, and the destruction of families. In order to achieve his aim, he brings:

The faithlessness

It leads fathers of over 60 years old to slave girls who are between 20 and 25 years. They spend all their fortune for these girls; they are ready to sacrifice everything *(money, material goods and women -children -work)* for these girls. Others leave the marital home to take refuge with them. This spirit leads some parents to hold sex with their own children. However married women feel at ease; this spirit causes them to have lovers *(adultery)*.

Seduction

The water spirit leads in this case the man or woman to seduce in order to drive him into sin by wearing sexy clothes *(darling look at my belly for example)*. Some women pierce their ears more than once, others the nose, the navel or the tongue. Men are also affected and there are even those who braid or uncurl their hair.

Sterility

Many couples divorced these days for lack of knowledge. This spirit makes some women infertile. May be after an intercourse in the dream, he removes the uterus or the fallopian of the woman. From that day, she becomes unable to conceive. The husband will find reasons to make children outside the marriage, what will lead to conflicts in the home *(result: The divorce)*.

I pray for all households living this case now that the Almighty GOD repairs the damage caused by this spirit and restore peace. Entrust your home to God; he is able to change your crying to joy and sterility into fecundity; in the name of Jesus Christ of Nazareth.

CHAPTER 4

THE WATER MERMAID *(MAMI WATA)* BASE OF MARITAL PROBLEMS

Definition: **Mami-wata** - *(Mami Wata)* or generally known under Mamiwata is a compound word composed of:

Mami = mother
Water = water

This means simply **mother of water.**
At night Mami attacks men while night husband attacks women. These two spirits are one of the greatest problems in the world *(in Africa and around the world).*

As I previously declared, many marriages nowadays are broken and several couples afflicted without well-founded reasons. This mermaid spirit hates unity and is itself very jealous. It likes to turn into its personal wealth the man or woman it possesses to expand its kingdom. That is the reason it tries to give the man or the woman an easy way to gain money and to make them believe they are happy. This spirit is pretending to enrich its prey to make them in the last days of their life to fall in desolation *(financial, celibacy, sterility, or bankruptcy.)* That is one of the reason, you will see men or women with successful businesses in the beginning but snap back to zero at the end.

This spirit causes hatred around you; your neighborhood will hate you without you offended them. Worst of all

22

those cases, your spouse too. This spirit which is renowned for the separation of couples injects a disease in the body of the woman *(sterility mostly)*. After analysis, we find that the fallopian tube of the woman is blocked, or there are other ailments such as ovarian cysts, fibroids, and myoma. That same spirit causes all negativity in all medical treatments to give a reason for the man to go take another woman out. It creates a strong tension in the home. For nothing, quarrels arise and intensify to the point where either the man abandons his wife and children, or he dismisses his wife. Remember that I said how this spirit possesses the body and in this case, consultation by fetish or marabouts to have a husband, wife or healing appears.

Let me tell you a true story that occurred following a trip I made to Ivory Coast. During a conference where I was invited as a speaker, the Lord told me about a woman who lost her menses for some time already. When I delivered the message, the Spirit of God shake her and she came up front. When I started to pray for her, the Spirit of God revealed to me the cause of her distress. She consulted a seer who supposedly predicted her that she will meet a man who would marry her. And before it is fulfilled, she had to buy a soap to take her bath with it and a perfume to attract the man *(because she will henceforth feel good)* also, yellow red and white candles with her photograph, her name and certain money.

After the woman has collected all the items listed above, the prophet has led her to a river for ceremonies that were required. The prophet after making her take all kinds of baths uttered incantations on elements together and returned the perfume and soap to the woman for use. Then, the prophet declared that before the soap and perfume are depleted, she will meet the man who will marry her. The woman was happy because the word of the seer had its fulfillment in the same month; she met the bone of her bones and flesh of his flesh, not knowing that she had just met the ordeal *(from her hell)* and the problem of her problems. The day the man put the ring on her finger, she lost her menses and this for two years, then I met her.

At that time, the husband had already decided to divorce her. I was led at the edge of the river that is in San Pedro. The woman was able to locate the place where the bath was taken, a tree grew there. We cut the tree and the Spirit of God prompted me to dig so, we dug. We discovered a talisman that contained the picture of the woman in pieces, a sheet on which was written a language which I had no knowledge. I burned everything and then I pray for the woman deliverance. In the same week, she found her menses. Remember that she was seeking child during those two years; doctors diagnosed every sickness remedies except those that were needed.

Let me present to you a very special person; did you know that those who invented the drug to cure malaria can be washed away by this disease? Are you aware of that the inventor of the airplane may die of the same device? Wait a moment, the one who invented the car can die from a car accident, the coffin maker necessarily becomes the client of honor of his work one day.

But there is a man who is the creator of heavens and earth. The Bible says that when he lived on earth, he terrorized Satan; when he died, he snatched the key of salvation from the death; Jesus Christ of Nazareth is his name.

Give your life to Jesus Christ and he will rejuvenate you again. Come to him, regardless of what you are going through, he is the maker of the impossible. What is already hopeless in your life? Come closer to him and you will realize that he never disappoints.

How many times did you do occult consultations? What was given to you to use? You must break the negative influence of those things in your life. Do you still have amulets or chemicals in your room? Burn them; if you cannot burn them, come to us and we will help you.

I met a paralyzed man who listened to one of my radio prayers. After that I called to pray for him. The Spirit of God told me that he buried things in his house and that is the basis of his paralysis. He let me know that it was a human skull that had cost him millions. Thereafter we dug up this human skull. The same night when he was sleeping he had a dream and saw a man dressed in white who came to massage both of his feet. In the morning, he woke up and started running. Glory to God!

Beloved, if you have chance to read this book, seize this opportunity to make peace with your GOD and he will grant you the miracle you seek.

CHAPTER 5

HOW TO RECEIVE AND MAINTAIN THE DELIVRANCE FROM THE WATER MERMAID?

Definition: **Deliverance** - The action of being rescued or set free. It is one thing to be rescued or set free and another thing to stay delivered.

How to receive rescue?

The first step is a self-deliverance; many people look for deliverance but forget the deliverer. The man of GOD will be a channel through which the Lord will act; but you, you have the duty to fix your eyes on GOD.

You must identify or locate the demons that are worrying you; it is the only way through which you can really be delivered. If you do not know the sickness you suffer of, it will be difficult even impossible to find the appropriate remedy. You can ask yourself the question how can you identify them? Make sure you use the pathway of that spirit *(mentioned above)*. We must seek the cause or the entrance way of those spirits in your life. Let's take the example of a thief who comes to steal in a house, but the gate is closed. The thief is inevitably forced to create a passage that the owner does not know. In order to solve this, it will be essential to discover this passage and close it. Most of the time, the entrance way of the demons in our life is our sin. **Proverbs 28: 13"he who conceals his transgressions (sins) shall not prosper, but whoever confesses and forsakes them shall have mercy."**

Five fields of fight

Confession of sins committed by oneself

Most of our parents worship different GODS *(demons-water-mountains, forests spirits, ancestors' spirits, etc...)* and many of them have put their family and even the future of the descendants under the control of these divinities. They made promises to these demons, the word that our parents passed before these fetishes gives them a legal right on us. Parents may die but the demons continue their dirty work. Since you are part of the family, your name is on the execution list. The Bible says that GOD punishes iniquity of the fathers upon the children unto the third and fourth generation.

The only way to be delivered or to be rescued from the family that you are affected with by alliance is to receive and accept Jesus Christ as Lord and Savior.

Confession of sins committed by parents

To achieve this, you need to get information on fetishes worshiped in your family, as well as the abominable practices that make them. Once you have gathered all these elements, you will mention them one by one in your prayer for their cancellation by the blood of Jesus; you will ask Jesus Christ to put a barrier between you and these demons and he will do it. Identify the names of all the fetishists, marabous and divinities known in the world. This may be shocking for you but it is an irreversible reality; you may tell me that you do not need to know all these names. This would be a serious mistake you would commit. It is not for nothing that by your first consulting of a fetishist or a witch doctor or marabou, he asks you your name; it is rather in order to maintain their dominance over your life and your soul is invoked many times by name to make you come back for their services. You must list everything you have given them for any sacrifice on your behalf *(silver, cloth, egg, chicken, sheep, etc...).*

You have to remember everything they made you drink, passed on any part of your body or buried or eaten *(cola nuts).* Confess them and asked that these things do not meet in your place because it is an unconsciously established alliance. Use the blood of Jesus Christ based
on **Galatians 3: 13 "Christ redeemed us from the curse of the law, being made a curse for us for it is written: cursed is everyone who hangs on a tree"** to cancel the alliance. **We must pray with authority** based on **Mark 16: 17 "these signs will accompany those who believe: In my name, they will cast out demons; they will speak new languages".**

Closing the front doors

Many people return to zero after being delivered because they have not closed the door. When an unclean spirit goes out, he does not rest; he remains in the surrounding so to learn about the current state of the house. Let take this example: "Night husband demon, I cast you out in the Name of Jesus Christ of Nazareth! For the cloth that I gave to fetish, you had access to my life and because I have already confessed him out of my life in the name of Jesus Christ! From now go I break this alliance and I shut the door. "

The restoration

Joel 2:25-27 "I will restore to you the years that the locust devoured, the cankerworm, and the caterpillar, and the palmer-worm, my great army which I sent among you. You will eat and you shall be satisfied, and you will praise the name of the LORD your GOD, who would have made you squanderers: and my people shall never be ashamed. And you will know that I am in Israel that I am the LORD your GOD, and there is none else, and my people shall never be ashamed"

Ask God to arrange everything that those spirits destroyed in your life, taking the decision never to do it again. If you are really tired of living under the influence of these spirits, you have to take a step towards to Jesus Christ. You can be rescued by fasting and prayer under the direction of a servant of GOD for a definitive freedom. But remember that nothing can be done if you do not take the necessary decision about your case. It is now up to you, brother, sister to decide about your fate. The Bible says in **Job 22: 28 "you shall also decree a thing, and it shall be established to you: and the light shall shine on your ways."**
What are you waiting for? Take a step toward Jesus Christ of Nazareth. He has dominated the things of this world. In

his name, all knees should bend and everybody should confess that He is Lord. You need to be guided by prayers and your life will be renewed. We are ready to help you to engage with Jesus of Nazareth. The Prophet Isaiah said "the **Spirit of the Lord GOD is upon me, because the Lord has ointed me to bring good news to the poor, he sent me to heal the broken in heart, for to proclaim liberty to the captives, and release to captives" (Isaiah 61: 1).**

Come to Jesus Christ, HE is calling you.

CHAPTER 6

WITCHCRAFT AND EFFECTS

Definition: **Witchcraft** is the practice of witches; but who can be called a witch?
A witch is a person who practices a traditional, a secret and illegal or dangerous traditional magic. If there is an area in which many people suffer because of ignorance; it is the one of witchcraft because it is a practice veiled of mysteries.

Witchcraft is one of the most dangerous departments in the satanic kingdom. It is distressing to see that witchcraft activities continue in many families without any challenge. What saddens me most is that there is a range of many destinies, countless souls have perished. Those who should be behind are at the front, several homes are broken, and a spell is cast on many people.
When I talk about challenge, you can ask yourself what it is about. What does the Bible say about?
Exodus 22: 18 "you will not let a witch live". Isaiah 49: 24-26 "will the loot of the mighty will kidnapped? And will the catch on the right escape? Yes, says the Lord, the catch of the mighty shall be taken away, and the prey of the terrible will escape him; I will fight your enemies, and I will save your people. I will make your oppressors eat their own flesh, they will be drunken with their own blood as with sweet wine, and all flesh shall know that I am the Lord your Savior and your Redeemer, the Mighty of Jacob."

There is a reality that you need to know: take the case of my country, BENIN every family has at least one wizard or witch, hence we have family wizards. When you are attacked by a family wizard, you are more easily accessible as if the wizard were out of the family. That's why most wizards look to have service colleagues in their group as benchmarks to operate efficiently in the life of the individual.

During their night meeting, the member of the family comes with information that will facilitate their action.

Example: You have a planned trip and this witch of the family was informed of your journey and has known in advance your success in the host country. He will inform his colleagues to stop you. I have always said that, all those who interact with you are not all your friends. They are witches who are with you during the day as friends, in ignorance you give them all your secrets. At nightfall, this witch meets about your case to destroy you then will have the nerves to sympathize with you in your sufferings. What an audacity!

The greatest sickness of man is ignorance.

Ignorance is the lack of knowledge; it is to be unconscious to learn; it is a lack of information. It is the basis of destruction. As long as you do not realize the reality of the existence of witchcraft, ruin will become your purpose. Some people are veiled by sorcerers, what lead them to look away from them for the cause of their misfortune. The witch who keeps a child in her womb for nine months does not hesitate to sacrifice him. Why do you seek to negotiate with them? As long as these witches live, the whole family will be immersed in the afflictions of sicknesses, infertility, inability to marry, professional failure, several anomalies and disastrous events. You must fight them like a wounded lion because they have the power to destroy to the fourth generation. For instance, if your great grand Father was a sorcerer, they can destroy from his generation, your father's, yours, and your children. They often sign pacts of 50 years renewable according to their testimony.

There is a lady who does not get along at all with her sister in law, because the latter does not want her as his brother's wife *(she is a witch sister in law)*. After many years of infertility, the lady had at last given birth to a child. The woman went to her servant one day and gave instructions to feed the baby with baby bottle when he awoke, and keep the remaining in the freezer. Instead of depositing the bottle in the freezer, the servant deposited the child there. Do not be surprised, this is not her fault, it is rather a manipulation from witchcraft. Result: the child died; the desire of the sister in law was accomplished.

Their means of contact

Their mean of contacts is among others: the owls, the rooks trees, the sun, the moon, the stars and the sand. You may be surprised that the moon and stars are mentioned but, you must know that the mermaid has its home in the sea and witchcraft is based in the first and second heaven. This is why we speak of astral trip. Their power ends in the second heaven, but God self-governs in third heaven with his angels and GOD says "the earth is my footstool." This means that his feet pierce the second and the first heaven, he rules over all these forces. For it to be so for you, you must give your life to the Lord.

Many people attribute witchcraft to old people, these people must get the reality because the world has changed, witchcraft too. Witchcraft is now targeting children from six to eleven years old, as well as older people. For instance, you hire a servant in your house without consulting a man of God for guidance, you will rather pay a wizard or witch for your hiring decision. Unknowingly, you pay for your own ruin. We encounter several of these cases everyday in Africa.

You must get up and strike your name from their list. Perhaps you now live in the same house, same room, same neighborhood or exercising the same job with a sorcerer; Call the fire! As soon as you are inflamed, this wizard cannot resist because darkness and light cannot live together. He will move away because of your presence. Make often aggressive prayers and your life will be a one-way for wizards.

CHAPTER 7

REVOKE THE DECREES OF WITCHCRAFT

Definition: The word **decree** is defined by an opinion expressed with a certain authority, it is a sentence; it is something that comes from the heart with authority. It is a judgment, an order, or an official decision.

In many places in the Bible, we find evil decrees pronounced on the children of GOD. Let's consider the case of Mordecai, a decree was pronounced on Mordecai and his people, decree that says his race will be exterminated at a fixed date.

What happened then? God has not only canceled the said decree, but he has also ruled the substitution of it. At the end of that day, Haman was hanged at the place reserved for Mordecai. This is what God has planned for wizards who always trouble you by leaving their bodies and transform your peace in disarray.

Daniel was also a victim; an evil decree came out about him; decree banning prayer of the living GOD **(Daniel 6)**. The authors of this word knew that Daniel could not retain himself from prayer to his GOD. They knew that that was the only way Daniel could fail. For having broken the law, he was thrown into the lions' den. Those who have committed this act experienced the fate planned for Daniel meaning they became the breakfast, lunch, and dinner of the lions. The same will be the destiny of the sorcerers who refuse to let you live in peace.

We are talking of the decrees of witchcraft and as you know, witchcraft is a science that works in darkness. They are very common these days and are eight in number (08), evil decrees which fight against GOD's children:

1- Curses.
2- Magic.
3- Incantations.
4- Spells.
5- The Satanic decisions.
6- The Satanic judgments: this occurs when a person is brought to evil court and in this case a judgment will be ruled at the end.
7- Satanic enchantments.
8- People endowed with strong evil.

These decrees are executed when your case is exposed to the evil world. In most of the cases, the dreams are the means of implementation of these decrees, for this reason it is important to remember dreams and nightmare to destroy sorcerers' phases. To execute their decision, these sorcerers invoke the spirit of man since witchcraft is a spiritual matter. By bringing the spirit of a person out of his body, then they pronounce the appropriate incantations on human life when he is asleep. That is the reason many are oppressed, fight, followed or ate in their dreams.

More over some people respond to their call in sleep *(dream)* or even awake even though nobody has really called them. Once you answer this mean you gave your agreement to the execution of a decree on your life. Problems will then follow each other; do you pray before you sleep? It is very necessary.

A sister heard her name three times in her sleep; so, she woke up naked and replied, stood up next to her husband and went out. This was the beginning of her madness, she became very crazy.

Wizards decided to kill a brother by the noise of the drums; they bring up the brother's face on the drums and start typing, and the swelling of his face would lead in the sickness and finally to death. They tried once and it did not clap. The second time, Jesus Christ himself appeared and they refused. In the third trial, the brother's face appeared and they were glad, they took a stick to knock him out when the brother's face changed into of one of them *(witches)*. Because of the momentum already taken, they were forced to hit the face there. Thus, the wizard died the next day because of the hits received.

If the wizards do not reach the aim at their disposal, they will attack your business. That is the reason, it is necessary to cover your business with the blood of Jesus Christ or they will turn you into a worthless.

What order did they take against you? What award or decision did they conclude? Jesus Christ is ready to turn it against them. That is why God has given us a ministry of spiritual fight. For example, every Friday from 7 p.m. we do aggressive intense prayer session called «Fire Blow

Operation". We slap, tear off the teeth and jaws of these wizards working. You need to join us for this great moment of victory. I mean every Friday from 7 p.m. to 9:00 p.m. Your victory is sure. Wizards will be under your feet in the name of Jesus Christ of Nazareth.

CHAPTER 8

A WEAPON OF WITCHCRAFT: THE DREAMS HOW TO OVERCOME SATANIC DREAMS?

Definition: The **dream** by definition is a natural way the spiritual world explodes in real life. It can also be known as a dark speech of the spirit. It is also a mean of revelation. The dream is one of the ways through which the Lord communicates with his children
Job 33: 14-16 "GOD speaks however, sometimes trough one way, sometimes trough another, and we are not aware of it. He talks in dreams, in night vision when men are engaged in a deep sleep, when they are asleep on their couch. Then he gives them warnings and puts the seal on his instructions" Acts 2: 17 "in the last days, says God, I will pour out my Spirit on all flesh; your sons and your daughters shall prophesize, your young men shall see visions, and your old men shall have dreams".

There are two types of dreams which are: dreams from God and those from the devil. But what concerns us here is the second category that is the **satanic dream.** Satanic dreams have only mission to destroy our lives by respecting sorcerers plan (**Matthew 13: 25**).

What is deplorable is that many people give no importance to their dreams. You agree with me that any normal person should sleep. All that God has created for man is for his interest. The sleep is not a bad thing. To help Adam, God made him fall into a deep sleep before taking out his side. The devil being a professional trickster also requires dreams to execute his plans. You must know that all that happens in the physical world is a reflection or the result of decisions taken in the spiritual world. They want to succeed in their mission.

Wizards make their victims forget the dreams. This is very dangerous to have dream and forget the purpose of the dream. The real purpose to make you forget your dreams is to forge malefic alliances with innocent souls. The wizard can use the body of a person you know well, or a parent or a relative to meet you while you sleep.

In order to spread sickness in some bodies, sorcerers will give them food in their sleep and make cure of such diseases impossible. There are people who are seriously ill, and have done every analysis but the result is always negative. The same wizards confuse the material system so the sickness will not be detected.

It is very important to remember dreams because God may want to warn you of danger planned in the enemy group against you. Therefore, you need to pray for deprogramming.

Some examples of dreams

- If you have once dreamed counting money this will result in poverty. You can find money, but it will not remain in your hands. No achievement.

- If you are breastfeeding a child in your dream or if you give birth in your dream, even if you see yourself in your dream pregnant the result is sterility.

- If you see yourself in the process of writing test in a classroom you have already attended for years, the result is that your life will be delayed.

- If you dream you see a parent, friend or acquaintance who has already died, or someone you do not even know, but who has the appearance of a death, the result is the spirit of death lurking around you.

- If you often dream and you see yourself in your hometown or your family home, you should know that there is a family connection that is causing you problem.

- If you dream you are eating, then you must know that either witchcraft was given to you or unknowingly injected disease in your body.

- Worst! There are people who dream and in the morning, they find they have urinated in bed, this is witchcraft.

CHAPTER 9

OVERCOMING ANTI-MIRACLES FORCES
(SPIRITS WATING BEHIND THE DOOR OF YOUR MIRACLE)

Definition: A **door** is an access way to a location or a place. In other words, it is a passage that allows us to leave a place to another.

Let's read the Bible in **1 Corinthians 16:9 "for a great door with an efficient access is opened to me and there are many adversaries."**

The gates in question in this text are the gates of blessings, achievements, joy. The Apostle Paul says, " for a great door with an efficient access is opened to me" and there are many adversaries. You must know that every time we have a special grace from the Lord, opponents appear. It simply means that whenever an opportunity presents itself to you, the opponents also point. This is an undeniably immutable truth to talk of evil forces or powers that await the opening of divine favor doors to lift. That's why you will see some people who suffer for long, but when everything seems to normalize in their life, an unexpected tragedy strikes them.

We frequently see these cases. Some just after finishing the construction of their home do not spend a single night before death visits them. Others only receive their first salary and there is a downfall that follows. You should know that behind all these events are the opponents waiting at the door like a lion. So, know that you have enemies that are invisible until the hands touch something vital, something that can change your destiny to hit. Take the case of Jacob, he saw the family wickedness knock on his door when his father blessed him, and this forced him to exile.

Genesis 27: 41-42 "Esau held a grudge against Jacob because of the blessing his father had given him. He said to himself, "The days of mourning for my father are near; then I will kill my brother Jacob." When Rebekah was told what her older son Esau had said, she sent for her younger son Jacob and said to him, "Your brother Esau is planning to avenge himself by killing you."

Many are experiencing such situation today simply because they laid the first stone of their house, programmed their marriage or because a door opened before them. The basis of these forces is family and their derive witchcraft. One of the main reason many projects are abandoned by their organizers.

<u>Example</u>: A young African living in Europe came to the country to meet his future stepmother and to do the engagement ceremony. He even started building a house in the country here, promising his return to his bride for the wedding. He disappeared for seven years and even was unreachable during that time. The problem was an aunt of the bride decided never to see them celebrate the

said marriage. Know who you tell your secrets; none of the girls of this aunt was proposed for marriage so, she does not want marriage for her niece by jealousy.

Psalm 127: 4-5 says "like arrows in the hand of a warrior, so are the children of the youth; Wealthy be the one who filled his quiver! they shall not be ashamed, when they shall speak with the enemies at the door.

You are like an arrow in the hands of the great warrior and you will not be afraid in front of the enemies at the gate. For years, you have been expecting the opening of a door *(business, wedding work, etc...)* do you know that the doors listen and speak? **In Psalm 24: 7-8, the bible says "doors, lift your lintels; lift, everlasting doors! That the King of glory may come in! Who is this King of glory? The Lord strong and mighty, the LORD, mighty in battle."** The Psalmist spoke to the doors and they listened. That is why they responded "who is this King of glory"?

If the doors listened and responded to the Psalmist, then you can talk to doors that are closed by the bad evils spirit on your life. Have Authority on all the resistances of these doors. Do you want a job? Speak to the door of employment and order it to open to you. Do you want to marry, talk to the door of marriage to open and let your spouse in? Do you want a business support; GOD will bring into existence what you have said.

For years, you have been complaining in front of your miracle door. You cry, you moan, this is not the solution. Your crying cannot change anything; on the contrary it is in difficult times that you are going to use the word of God to find concrete results. God gives you the opportunity to break down the doors locked in front of you, so that you may leave the negative, failure to complete victory.

By reading this book, take a decision because the Bible says whatever you bind on earth will be bound in heaven.

CHAPTER 10

YOUR DESTINY FACED
TO FAMILY WITCHCRAFT

In this theme, we have some keywords that we must explain first:

• **The Destiny**

This is GOD's plan for your life, it is the future that God has prepared in advance for you. This is what you will be or what you are already.

If you are not in your destiny for instance, you must get up to look and find out God's plan for your life in order to achieve your destiny. If you are already in your destiny, know that this is not an end because there is around you jealous people *(the destiny killers)*; try your best to keep it. In summary, your destiny is what you are born for; this is what God had in his heart before creating you and sending you on earth. This is what God has written in his guest book about you. In many places in the Bible, Jesus told us about his destiny "man's son goes as it is written." Listen, Pierre wanted to stop Jesus from reaching his destiny but Jesus did not allow him, he turned and said, behind me Satan!

You need to get upset against any power opposed to the realization of what is written about you in the guestbook **Jeremiah 29: 11 "for I am with you", the LORD said** "to deliver you, I will destroy all nations within which I have scattered you, but you, I will not destroy you. I will chasten you with fairness, I cannot let you go unpunished". Jeremiah 1: 5 "before I formed you in the womb of your mother, I knew you and before you came out of her womb I sanctified you, and I ordained you a prophet of the nations."

• **The Family**
This is a group of people composed of father, mother, and children. We can also include aunts, uncles, grandparents etc... We cannot talk about family without mentioning the home.

•**The Home**
It is a home, it is a place of ordinary residence, a legal and habitual residence it is an accommodation. It is the domestic unit that includes all family members living together.

• **The Witchcraft**
Its meaning in Greek is python, python is a large snake called destroyer. The destroyers kill their preys by suffocating slowly. In the same way, the spirit of Python tries to suffocate people to confuse their destiny. In the word witchcraft *(wizard)* we must lie or change people and their situation into the worse. This is the home of the coordination wish the devil. **John 10:10 "steal, kill and destroy"** it is the weapon used by Satan to make and break. But the Bible says that Jesus the son of God

appeared to destroy the works of the devil.

Speaking of destiny in the face of home witchcraft, family wickedness is the basis. The people who were supposed to be the head are now the tail. Those who were supposed to have children are sterile, those destined for marriage are single. Included, those who should have their own business, house car, etc.... found themselves at the bottom of the ladder and they wonder what sin they committed to deserve this? They seek the cause of their misfortune far from them, when the Bible clearly indicates that everyone will have enemies from his own house. Thus, begin your researches from your own house, my friend. Every man is born with its star. The star is about your present and your future. There are members of your family who do not want you to overtake them or their children. For this, a spiritual battle bears, **Genesis 4: 8-12 "it is here about two brothers out of the same breast, Cain and Abel; both offered to GOD and GOD has approved Abel's offering and rejected that of Cain. In other words, Abel has benefited of God's blessing. Hate and jealousy drove his brother Cain to kill him."**

Remember that God's blessings and the destiny of a man does not depend upon his family position. Cain was the eldest and Abel the youngest, both were born of Eve. They stayed in the same belly but was not born to have the same destinies. Take the case of twins Esau and Jacob and stop seeing the destiny from what your parents have lived or relative to your current situation. You can go to bed this night and the day that will rise tomorrow will shine the brightness of your star through the sun to fulfill your destiny. In **Genesis 4: 10 the Lord said to Cain "why did you do that? I hear the blood of your brother crying out for vengeance."** Your star will cry for vengeance and the soil in which it was buried will be forced to vomit it, in the name of Jesus.

Do you not want to build your own house, having children, traveling like the others, to have money to make great achievements like the others? One thing is required: call on God to shine the brightness of your star that represents your destiny. Today we see many zémidjan drivers *(motorbike taxi)* who have already made brilliant studies, they speak refined French but with no job. To avoid being public danger, they choose to drive by force zémidjan for a living and to support themselves.

Get up! Surely someone may be on the road to your destiny and blocks your evolving. But I assure you that by the aggressive prayer, that person will be moved so that you enter the circle of your destiny. That's why, every day that God makes, I pray in this way "anyone who enters the circle of my fate is toasted by the fire of the Holy Spirit in the name of Jesus Christ of Nazareth"!

Can you join me? You will get by all means the result you want. Your life will change in the name of Jesus Christ of Nazareth!

CHAPTER 11

THE SEVEN METHODS FOR A SUCCESSFUL PRAYER

The real intercessors are often neither seen nor known, nor approved of men, but God sees them, knows them and approves them. They are the first target of the devil but at the same time, they are apple of the eye of the LORD. The Intercessors are recognized by their humility, their gentleness, their life of love of holiness and especially of their intense prayer life **Genesis 18: 16-33, "the men rose up to go, and looked toward Sodom side, Abraham went with them to accompany them" then the Lord said: "will I hide from Abraham what I am going to do?" LORD went his way, when he had finished speaking with Abraham. And Abraham returned to his home."**

Exodus 32: 9-14, the Lord said to Moses: "I see that people are a stiff-necked people, now leave me alone, that my wrath may burn them and I will consume them, but I will make of you a big nation and the LORD repented of the evil which he intended to do with his people".

The conquering prayer is a prayer that has the power to entertain GOD to change decision and to revoke the satanic decrees.

- **First Method**

The prayer of fasting: what is it?

To fast is to deprive oneself of eating, drinking and all pleasures for a period and for a specific purpose. There is no noble price for fasting, then one does not fast for a record or to show off. Fasting is one of the most suitable positions for the favor, help, assistance intervention and GOD miracle. **Esther 4: 15-17, "Esther sent to tell to Mordecai; go gather all the Jews who are in Susa, and fast for me, and neither eat nor drink three days, night or day with my maids and I will enter to the king despite the law; and if I am to perish, I will perish, Mordecai went and did all that Esther had ordered him."**

Many Christians neglect fasting hence, all those who have made achievements in the Bible took this way, **Exodus 24: 12-18, the Lord said to Moses "come up to me on the mountain, and be there I will give you tablets of stone, the law and decrees which I have written for their instruction". Moses rose with Joshua and Moses went on the mountain of God.**
Moses went into the midst of the cloud, and went up on the mountain; Moses was on the mountain forty days and forty nights.

Fasting allows us to have a superior mind; it makes us mature, victorious and gives us the ability to face any situation and reverse in our favor. It allows us to humble ourselves better and to mortify our bodies so that GOD has easy access to our life. It is impossible to go into the depths of God without Fasting life. **Matthew 17: 21, "but this kind evil goes out but by prayer and fasting."** There are some mountains that move only in fasting.

- **<u>Second method</u>**

The prayer of faith

Pray with faith is:
- To speak a word with conviction
- Make a strong statement,
- Prophesy positively
- Confessing victoriously
- Say a word with boldness
- Bring to life through the word which does not exist and believe that,
- Enact to revoke an existing decree.

The prayer of faith is often short and spontaneous, it is believing in what you say or do. When we are faced with a danger or difficulty, we must pronounce a word of faith or make a prayer of faith.

Exodus 14: 13-14, Moses answered to the people: "fear not, stand still and see the salvation the LORD will give you this day, for the Egyptians you see today you will never see them again".
Joshua 10: 12-19, then Joshua spoke to the Lord, in the day when the LORD delivered up the Amorites to

the children of Israel, and he said in the sight of Israel "sun, stand still over Gibeon and moon, in the valley of Ajalon and you do not stop, follow up your enemies and attack from behind; do not let them enter into their city, for the LORD your God has delivered them in your hand."

The Word of God invests us with a strength and power by which we have a spiritual authority that allows us to change all situations, circumstances and obstacles that lie ahead.

- **Example of Hezekiah who pronounced a word of faith, confidence, and determination in the heart of his people by reassuring them of victory that God will grant them, 2 Chronicles 32: 5-8.**

- **Example of the Apostle Paul who reassured by word of faith who were with him in the ship, Acts 27: 21-22.**

- **Example of Joshua stopped the sun's and moon than anything from a spoken word, Joshua 10: 12-14.**

- **Example of David who says to Goliath he would kill him and cut his head off 1 Samuel 14: 45-50.**

- **Third method**

The prayer of fight

It is the prayer of deliverance, of deprogramming, of liberation, recovery, of release, power force, war, poverty, and brokenness. It is only focused on the devil, its demons, its evil spirits, its visible and invisible agents, its works, and its empire. A Christian who does not fight cannot experience victory because there is no victory without a fight.

Every family on this earth has received the visitation of the devil in one way or in another and we all know it comes only to destroy, block and tie. For the efficiency of the battle of prayer, we must bring spiritual weapons as the Bible says **in Ephesians 6: 10-18 "to the rest, be strong in the Lord and in the all-powerful force. Put the whole armor of God, to be able to stand against the wiles of the devil. Do at all times in the Spirit, with all prayer and supplication. Please to do this with all perseverance and supplication for all saints."**

- **Fourth method**

Intercessory prayer

Intercede is:
- Advocate for a cause
- Defend a culprit
- Supplier
- Submit queries and complaints

- Attract the favor, compassion, forgiveness, and mercy of God on a family, a nation or an individual,
- Dunning GOD
- Pray with patience, persistence, perseverance until fulfillment. **Luke 18: 1-8, Jesus spoke a parable to them, to show that we must always pray and not relax. I tell you "he will avenge them speedily, but when the son of man cometh, shall he find faith on the earth?"**

Intercession is of great importance in the church, the nation; when a church lack of intercession, spiritual bankruptcy, division, and spiritual death settles. It automatically becomes the benchmark and prey witches vampires and criminals. Intercession can bring change, restoration, power, life, glory of God in a church as well as in a home and in a nation. The church intercessors must therefore be serious and know their own role. An intercessor should not criticize, judge or condemn. His mission is to plead, cry, moan and implore the grace of God until the change. The intercessor is a defense attorney, a guard, a sentry, a repairer.

- **Fifth method**

The prayer of votive

This is to request something from God with a promise;
- Request by taking a sacred commitment,
- Pray putting God in test,

- A Challenge prayer.

This is the fastest and most efficient method that can exist because it forces God to act even if he did not want it:
- Stimulates GOD
- Moves the sky
- Attracts GOD attention in a particular way. There is a power, a miracle, a mystery, unwavering strength, and unbreakable vow in prayer. This prayer is not done anyhow; it is recommended that in critical cases.

1 Samuel 1: 10-11, and the bitter in soul, she prayed the Lord and wept; She made a vow, saying "Lord of hosts! if you now look on the affliction of your handmaid, if you remember me, and not forget your handmaid, and if you give to your handmaid a male child, then I will give him to the Lord all the days of his life, and no razor will never come upon his head."

The vow displaces God, even he does not displace himself anyhow because his movement is still terrible and healthy. We must therefore not make vow to God anyhow. The case of Jephthah is a concrete example. Making prayers of vow is also experimenting GOD, it makes the heart of GOD sensitive and flexible.

Judges Chapter 11; Genesis 28: 20-22 "Jacob made a vow saying, If God is with me and keep me in this trip I make, and if he gives me bread to eat and cloth to wear, and if I return in peace to my father's house, then

the LORD will be my God; this prayer, which I have set for a pillar, shall be God's house; and I will give you dime of everything you give me."

- <u>Sixth method</u>

Remembrance or referential prayer

It is a monument or a giant note that every believer must draw or place to let it be his support and witness between heaven and him and vice-versa.

The prayer of remembrance is also one of the most efficient and terrifying methods that may exist. It is to make a monument or an act in relation with God to his work, his children, and his servants. Remembrance prayer is powerful because it changes the mind to God; it overturns decisions taken by GOD himself about an individual, a person or a nation.

In principle, every Christian should have his name written in the book of remembrance so to make reminders to God in his time to benefit from his saving intervention. Many people cry out to God today, but their prayer has no support because they have nothing to get GOD attention or to touch his throne. It is very important for every Christian to invest in the work of God by taking actions that will be a testimony of monuments whose memory will bring God to bless us or decant a situation in due time. King Hezekiah is a concrete example in the Bible. **2 Kings 20: 2-6, Hezekiah turned his face against the wall and**

prayed to the Lord: "Ô Lord remember that I have walked in front of you with faithfulness and heart probity, I did what is good in your eyes and Hezekiah burst into tears." Isaiah who has gone out, was not so far as the word of the LORD came to him in these words back and tell Hezekiah the captain of my people. Thus, said the LORD, David your father "I have heard your prayer, I have seen your tears, behold, I will heal you, the third day you shall go to the house of the LORD. I will add unto your days fifteen years. I will deliver you, you, and this city out of the hand of the king of Assyria,
I will defend this city for my sake and for David my servant."

Nehemiah 13: 14-22, "remember me, Ô GOD, because of this, and do not forget my acts of piety towards the house of my God and things that must be observed! I command also the Levites to purify themselves and come keep the doors to sanctify the Sabbath day. Remember me, Ô my GOD, because of this, and protect me according to your great mercy."

- <u>Seventh method</u>

Prayer by the praise and worship

There is nothing that God loves and cherishes than praising and worshiping. The Bible tells us that God sits in the middle of the praise and worship. There is one thing that God cannot do, he cannot praise and worship himself.

To do this, we can say that eating, drinking and breathing are GOD praise and worship. Praising God seriously and deeply, we can be healed, delivered, receive full Holy Spirit, receive the gift of the Spirit and or explosion of his spiritual gift. No problem, no sickness and no difficulties can withstand someone who praises and worships God from his heart. **Acts 16: 25-34, in the middle of the night, Paul and Silas were praying and singing praises to God, and the prisoners heard them. Suddenly there was a great earthquake, so that the foundations of the prison were shaken, at the same time, all the doors were opened, and everyone bands were loosed. They were led into his house and served food, and he rejoiced with his whole house for having believed in God.**

Car, plane, boat or master that can lead someone into the presence of God are the praise and worship. It is also important to use this method and you will see the change from negative to positive. The curse will hand in blessing, the walls of your Jericho will crumble. Praise flourishes you and makes you the winner; Paul and Silas in prison, are palpable examples in the Bible.

The Bible says: in the middle of the night, while they were praising and worshiping the Lord the prison walls crumbled and the doors were shaken. You might be in a spiritual prison: sickness prison, celibacy, unemployment, debt, spell cast on you, etc... choose this method of prayer, apply, and see what God will do for you.

He will deliver you from this prison and you will give a testimony. Believe and you will see the glory of God manifesting in your life in the name of Jesus Christ of Nazareth.

CHAPTER 12

DEFEAT THE FORCES FIGHTING AGAINST YOUR MARRIAGE OR YOUR HOME

There is a reality that many people are suffering of today, the evil forces that attack homes. The devil injected in our generation evil forces struggling against marriages and who undertake to prevent people from marrying. These forces destroy the well-established homes by introducing financial difficulties and by bringing in sickness and death. The chaos in marriage is caused by evil forces. These forces are in the whole world. They control, manipulate, plunder and destroy the homes at a cruising speed. They often bring misunderstanding to separate the husband from his wife for no good reason. This separation is only the result of what was commissioned in the invisible by these forces. These same forces prevent some people from marrying. On some people, they put a label that makes them turn around without finding a spouse. In some cases, this is due to a family intervention (*gouges, scarification, family idols worship, divination consultations, etc...*).

If there is a fight the devil leads today with care and boldness that is the one against the home and marriage. Some parents also have planned their children even before they are born with fetishes (*dansi, Dansou, tronsi, etc...*). That is already a planned marriage. These children once they grow have difficulties to get married. Some couples seek stability and peace of their own home with witch doctors and marabouts. Man cannot give you what he has.

But the devil has neither peace nor stability; so, stop doing this charlatans alliance. The peace that the world seeks and does not find is the one Jesus gives. Many are those households who suffer today; the husband and his mother are sometimes associated to beat up the wife.

In other cases, the woman who suffered with her husband died suddenly at the time she would start enjoying the fruits of her patience. **Colossians 2: 14, he has expunged out the written orders that condemned and remained against us, and he destroyed it by nailing it to the cross. Galatians 3: 12-14, Christ redeemed us from the curse of the law, being made a curse for us, for it is written: cursed is everyone who hangs on a cross. So, that the blessing of Abraham might come on the Gentiles through Jesus Christ, and that we might receive the Spirit by faith that was promised.**

You who are about to separate from your husband or your wife, I advise you not to do this because I present someone who is the prosecutor of peace. Begin with prayer. No situation IS difficult and cannot resist to prayer. Difficult does not mean impossible. There is no marriage without problems; but the only way to dispel these problems without any trace is the use of scripts.

Let me tell you this reality too. Many households nowadays have problems due to lack of communication. There are other weddings that are not based on Jesus Christ who is the rock. In one word, many have not sought the face of God for their wedding, but the face of the man because of money, he is beautiful and vice versa. They threw themselves in marriage, marriage that is a no return path and today they are subject of harmful consequences. Do not worry in choosing your spouse because you must stay together for all your life. Know that there is a difference between speed and precipitation. GOD helps you understand this message. Money cannot buy happiness. Do not follow the money that your partner possesses and engage marriage with him. You may experience a poor and your union will make you a very rich torque because GOD has stood security for it.

Example: A pastor asked God to give him the love of his life. He prayed insistently. Twice he received a visit of two different women who are crippled. The Pastor accused the devil and he said all the time: back from me Satan, Satan you are defeated, the third time he met another as crippled and he sent her away as before; GOD warned him instantaneously "if you do so, you will die because it is my choice for you. He obeyed the voice of God." He took the woman and the two were married. She became pregnant and the day of birth, the child had difficulties to get out. The pastor prayed with insistence and sometimes later, when the child's head came out, both feet of women rallied (Glory to God)! No one had asked for the feet of the woman.

An American pastor heard this great miracle and the couple was invited to the United States to testify in over thirty churches. They returned very blessed (centenary of musical instruments with great fortune and subsidies for the pastor's church).

This is the result of his obedience, because without this woman, he could not get this great blessing. Keep seeing around you. Looks away and obeys the voice of God for your marriage and get the rewards.

AMEN!

CHAPTER 13

HOW TO TAKE CONTROL OF THE DAY?

Definition: The **day** is by definition a duration of time that covers from sunrise to sunset. The day is the clarity or light that the sun pours upon the earth. The day is of the night. The day is a challenge in the spiritual warfare.

It is a living reality that hears and speaks a language Psalm 19: 3-5. The day is able to speak for us or against us, in our favor or disfavor. When this happens, we say one day: "this or that happened." It can be a happy or unhappy event, the day would have thus spoken in our favor or disfavor. My prayer is that the day always defends our cause.

You will see in the Bible some men of God who pray on a specific day, that means their day of birth. Case of Job, Job 3: 1-10 and case of Jeremiah 20: 14. There is also an undeniable reality in the content of day, it has two doors, one indoor and an exit door. This explanation lies in the simple fact that we are entering a day and we can only enter where a door or an opening exists. The gateway of the day is between midnight and 3 a.m.; the day exit door is between five and seven in the evening (5 p.m. and 7 p.m.). The day thus has a void time that allows us to charge ourselves between seven and midnight or to review and make programs. To give you a comprehensive illustration, let's take the case of a closured house with a gate; there's a distance between the gate of the living room door and distance separates the living room door to backyard.

To take control of the day, take control of the front door and give him instructions. This happens between midnight and three in the morning. I it is for this reason also that night Travelers namely wizards do their bad drawing between midnight and three am.

Ladies and gentlemen, you must know these secrets: GOD has also given the power to bind and loose and the sky has only mission to deliver what you have said. In one word, you can through your word open a door or close it to your life (Colossians 4: 3-4). You can through prayer, your declaration can restore your life when it seems stacked or blocked.

Example: The opening of marriage doors, restoring of function of reproduction, fertility to exit the jails of infertility, opening the door to healing of sicknesses; access to a job or a deserved promotion. Opening the doors of a country by obtaining a visa, obtaining a degree to crown our work seriously, opening the doors of a project.

Let's consider the case of Paul and Silas in prison in Acts 16: 25-26, it is to this period that the main door of the day they were praying and singing when suddenly the foundations of the prison were shaken. All the doors opened and the chains that held captive prisoners fell. It is not necessary to pray for three hours' time; what is important is that the prayer is done in this time of night that marks the beginning of the day or even the return of the day.

Preparation

A Sincere repentance is required. If for example it is the opening a door for degree, we should confess to the Lord every time we have entrusted our academic and professional future to other gods different from him *(marabouts, fetish, spirits of ancestors, family geniuses etc...)*.

The steps of prayer

This is to fight the opposition gate so to destroy it.

Example: if we want the marriage, we must first fight the opposition door that is celibacy. In order to destroy it we must call the blood of Jesus and the fire of the HOLY SPIRIT. Read therefore Psalm 24:1-6.

We must then present to the LORD our innocent hands, and our pure heart; then let's give him our soul and remember him in our commitment to the truth. Let's request after that the door of marriage so that it opens and we may enter it with the GLORY of the LORD, the EVERLASTING, and Psalm 24: 7.

Let's come to GOD based on Genesis 2: 18 and let's claim for our spouse by going to meet him/her with a prayer based on Matthew 25: 1 and give thanks to God with Romans 8: 28. Psalm 5: 2 and 4: 3, Lamentations 22-23, Job 38: 12-15.

This passage from the Bible shows us that we can take authority or order the day. Job 38:14 tells us about clay, an earthy rock that can be molded when wet. When the potter takes the clay, he gives it the form he likes. The biblical evocation of the clay is the allusion to change or transformation confirming us that we are the potter of our own life.

We can change, in agreement with the Word of God, the day at our convenience and transform as the potter gives form to the clay, by focusing to date the garment of our choice. It is also necessary to pray to destroy the satanic plans contained in certain day so to prevent their execution.

Pray with Job 5: 12-14, Psalm 10: 15, Jeremiah 10: 11, and Psalm 45: 10-11, Isaiah 32: 1-2.

It does not consist of pronouncing or reading simply these verses but taking every word and customize it. After that, add your intentions as the psalmist had a specific state of mind, a definite position before writing each psalm, so add your personal requests and proclamations in accordance with Isaiah 55: 11.

CHAPTER 14

HOW TO TAKE CONTROL OF THE WEEK?

Definition: A **week** is a period of time composed of seven days.

According to the Bible, the first day of the week is Sunday. To take control of the week, we must succeed in taking control of the entrance gate of the first day. How does the first day of the week correspond to Sunday? Matthew 28: 1 says "after the Sabbath, at dawn on the first day of the week."
The Sabbath is Saturday and dawn after the Sabbath is undoubtedly Sunday. The version "sewer" of the Bible says "after the Sabbath, as the day began to join the Sunday morning."

Mark 16: 9 "JESUS risen early the first day of the week." So to take control of one week, we must act, not in the night of Sunday to Monday, but in the night of Saturday to Sunday between midnight and three in the morning. It is at that moment that the week takes birth like a baby; you can give it the shape you want, arrange its nose and ears to your choice, and so on. This is a good time to sow good seeds that will produce spiritual good fruits for seven days. The spiritual will then lead to the physical and the week will be positive for you.

Good spiritual seeds in question here are the words that come out of the mouth. Your word is a seed as the Bible has mentioned it. It is mainly for the control of the week that verse Psalms 19: 3 is used because if Sunday is instructed from you, he will communicate it to Monday, and so on.

Illustration: If the Chief Executive of a company wants to get a decision in his firm, he will inform his assistant, who at his turn will make the Chief of Staff aware and then the staff.

CHAPTER 15

HOW TO TAKE CONTROL OF THE MONTH?

Definition: A **month** is by definition each of the twelve divisions of the year; this is a space of time which is about thirty days.

Just like the day, the month has two doors namely the new moon and the full moon. Because of the posthumous works from handling of the month at is a creature of God by idolaters *(worships, rituals, etc...)*. It is proper as a child of God to place spiritual ambush two days before their arrival and clean the air two days after the disappearance to take control of the month. Since, Satanists take the moon to their God, they make it an idol and pollute the atmosphere of the month with their rituals.

The harmful danger of this act is to submit all those ignorant to the decision or the covenant they have signed with the moon for the month. However, the moon was created by God, the Creator of heaven and earth, you can talk to the moon under the authority that God has given you, telling him to listen to the voice of its creator. If Satanists do it and it obeys, how much less you who was mandated to dominate as a child of GOD must do it in the same way.

In this case, prayer should go against evil uses of the star that presides over the night. The star is a celestial body considered in relation to its impact on humans *(stars, astrology, planets, satellite etc...)*.

Example: The star of the day the sun. The world is made of stars and men.

Preparation

1- Repentance is necessary even indispensable especially compared to our relationship with the horoscope, the astrology and all our traditional beliefs and practices related to the sky, personally and specifically with the moon.

2- Giving thanks to God, he who gave you the opportunity to live and to see this month.

3- The steps of prayer *(See the control of the day)*.

CHAPTER 16

HOW TO TAKE CONTROL OF THE YEAR?

Definition: the **year** is a twelve-month period exactly corresponding to the time duration of the revolution of the earth around the sun. It is a period that includes two solstices and two equinoxes.

A solstice is both periods of the year when the sun reaches its greatest distance from the equator and is a maximum or minimum duration of the day in the northern hemisphere. We have the winter solstice which extends from 21st or 22nd December to 20th March and the summer solstice, which extends from 21st June to 20th September.

The Equinox is one of the two periods of the year when the day and night are the same duration because the sun crosses the equator. There is the spring equinox which is between March 21st and June 20th and the autumn equinox which is between 02nd September and 20th December.

Definitions have identified four words that we need to understand which are: Summer, winter, spring, and autumn.

- The Summer is the season which follows the spring and autumn above (21st or 22nd June).

- The Winter is the coldest seasons of the year and begins on 21st or 22nd December.
- The Spring is the first season of the year and begins on 20th or 21st March.

- The Autumn is the season which follows the summer and precedes the winter in the northern hemisphere (22nd or 23rd September).

The year's entrance halls are five in number, they are the solstices, equinoxes and New Year's Eve is December 31st of the year.
So to take control of the year, we need to guard these five entrances.

CHAPTER 17

SOME KEYS FOR BIBLE PRAYERS

1. Morning Prayer

Hear my words, O LORD ! Hear my moans! Hear my complaints with care! My King and my God! It is to you that I pray, Lord! You hear my voice! In the morning, I turn to you and I look; for you are not a God who has pleasure for evil; the wicked cannot dwell with you. LORD, lead me in your rightness because of my enemies; smoothed your way under my feet. Then all those who trust in you will rejoice; they will have joy forever and you will defend them. You will be a joy for those who love your name. For you bless the right, Ö Lord! You will load him with grace as a shield (Psalm 5: 2-5, 9, 12, 13).

My feet are firm in your paths, my feet don't slip. Indicates your goodness, you who saved those seeking refuge; protect me as the apple of your eyes, protect me in the shadow of your wings. Receive favorably the words of my mouth and the meditation of my heart, ö Lord, my Rock, and my Redeemer (Psalm 17: 5, 7, 8, 19, 15).

Lord! I lift my soul to you my God! I trust in you, I must not be ashamed!
All those who trust in you shall not be ashamed Lord! Let me know your ways, show me your paths, lead me in your truth and lead me for you are the God of my salvation,

you're still my hope, O Lord! Remember you of your mercy and goodness, for they are eternal (Psalm 25: 1-6).

Oh, God! You are my God, I am searching you, my soul thirsty for you. When I think of you, when I think of you on my bed, I meditate on you the whole night. For you are my help and I will rejoice in the shadow of your wings (Psalm 63: 2, 7-8).

2. Evening Prayer

Yours is the day, yours is the night, you have created the light and the sun; you have set all the borders of the earth, you have made summer and winter (Psalm 74: 16-17). Lift upon us the light of your face; ö Lord I go to bed and fall asleep in peace, for you alone, Lord Ö! You give me security in my home (Psalm 4: 7b, 9).

It is nice to praise the Lord and celebrate his name, Ô very nice to glorify your goodness in the morning and your faithfulness every night. You make me glad through your works, O Lord! And I sing with joy the works of your hands; how great are your works, O LORD, how deep are your thoughts!

A brutish man knows nothing about it; and the foolish does not fear. When the wicked spring as the grass, when all people of iniquity flourish, it is to be destroyed forever. But you are the almighty and forever; O Lord! (Psalm 92: 2, 3, 5, 9).

3. Prayer in temptation

Arise, O Lord God, raise your hand! Do not forget the poor! Why does the wicked despise God? Why does he say in his heart? Don't you punish? However, you look because you see the pain and suffering. So, to take up their case, the unfortunate abandons himself to you, you come to the aid of the orphan. You hear the wishes of those who are suffering, O Lord, you strengthen their heart. You listen to give right to the fatherless and the oppressed, so that the man of the earth may no more oppress (Psalm 10: 12, 14, 17, 18).

Lord! Hear my voice, I call upon you, have mercy on me and answer me! My heart says from you, seek my face! I seek your face, O Lord! Do not hide me your face, do not repel away with anger your servant! You are my help, do not leave me, and do not forsake me, God of my salvation! Look, Lord! Have mercy on me! Lord, help me! Lord, be not far from me! And my tongue will sing of your righteousness, it will praise you every day (Psalm 27: 7-9; 30:11; 35: 22b).

Have mercy on me, O God, have mercy on me! For in you my soul looks for refuge; I look for refuge in the shadow of the wings until the calamities have passed, rise upon the heavens, O God!

May your glory be poured above all the earth! Why do you hide your face? Why do you forget our affliction and oppression? Arise for our help! Deliver us to the causes of your goodness! (Psalm 57: 2, 5, 25, 27).

O God hear my voice when I groan! Protect my life against the enemy that I fear! Give us aid against distress! The Human Relief is only vanity Lord. You alone can help the weak as the strong come to our help, O Lord our God! For it is on you that we rely and have come in your name against this multitude. You are the one who possesses strength and power and that no one can resist?

We do not know what to do, but our eyes are on the roof. Save us, O God of our salvation, gather us and deliver us from the nations, to give thanks unto your holy name, and that we triumph in your praise (Psalm 64: 2; 60: 13; 1 Chronicles 14: 10, 20: 6b, 12; 1 Chronicles 16: 35).

Grant me Lord! For your mercy is huge. In your great mercy, turn your face to me and don't hide your face to your servant! Since I am in distress, bring me to raise up! Come near my soul, deliver it! Save it because of my enemies! I am poor and sorrowful: O God, Let me up! (Psalm 69: 17 – 19:30).

However, I am always with you, you hold me by my right hand lead me through your advice then you will receive me in glory. Who do I have in heaven but you? And on earth I only desire you; my flesh and my heart may fail, God is always the strength of my heart and my portion Psalm 73: 23-26).

Listen, O Shepherd of Israel, you who lead Joseph like a flock! Appear in your glory, you who is sitting on the cherubs! Come to our aid! O GOD. Restore us let your face shine, and we will be saved! Let your hand be upon the man of your right hand, upon the son of man that you're chosen! And we will move away more than you. Make us revive and we will call upon your name, O LORD God of hosts, restore us. Let your face shine, and we shall be saved! (Psalm 80:3b, 2, 418-20).

You will get up, you will comfort Zion, because the time to have pity on her time is fixed to an end; for your servants take pleasure in the stones, they will favor the dust. Then the nations will fear the name of the LORD, and all the kings of the earth, your glory. For the LORD shall build up Zion, he shall appear in his glory (Psalm 102: 14-17).

Lord, remember me in your kindness for your people! Remember me giving him your help, so that I may see the good of your chosen that I may rejoice in the joy of your people that I may glory with your inheritance! We have sinned with our fathers, we have committed iniquity, we have done wickedly, save us, Lord our God! So that we praise your holy name, and you put our glory in your praise (Psalm 106: 4-6, 47 a/c). I lift my eyes to you who seats in heaven, have mercy on us, Lord have mercy on us! For we are exceedingly filled with contempt, Lord, pour out your blessings on the good and those whose heart is right! (Psalm 123: 1, 3 125: 4).

Lord for years, God of Israel, sitting on the cherubs! It is you who is the only God of all the kingdoms of the earth, you have made heaven and earth. LORD, bow down your ear, and hear. Lord, open my eyes and look! Lord our God, deliver us from his hand, and all the kingdom of the earth may know that you alone are the LORD. Lord, so our captives, like streams in the South! (Isaiah 37: 16-17a-20; Psalm 126: 4).

Look down from heaven and see, from your holy and glorious remains: where is your zeal and your strength? The yearning of your heart and your compassion are no more towards me. However, you are our father, though Abraham does not know us, and Israel does not know who we are, LORD is our father, who is from everlasting is our savior. Why, O LORD, do you make us wander from your ways and harden our heart against your fear? Return for your servant's sake, the tribes of your heritage! Your holy people have possessed little time, our enemies have trodden down your sanctuary. We have long been like a people that you do not rule over and who are called by your name.

Oh! If you would rend the heavens and come down, the mountains might quake at you as a dry fire wood light, as if the bubbling water evaporates. Your enemies would know your name, and the nations tremble before you. When you didst terrible things which we did not expect, you came down and the mountains quaked at you.

It has been never learnt or heard, and the eye has never seen any God but you did such things for those who entrusted to him. You go to one who joyfully practices justice, those who walk in your ways and remember you.

But you were angry, because we have sinned, and we suffer long until we are saved.

We are all as unclean thing and all our righteousness as filthy rags. We are all fade as a leaf, and our iniquities, like the wind takes us away. There is no one who calls on your name, who wakes up to approach you. That is why you covered our face, and let us die by the effect of our crimes.

But now, O LORD, you are our father, we are the clay and you have shaped us, we are the work of your hands. Do not get nervous at most O Lord, and do not always remember the crime; So, look we are all your people (Isaiah 63: 15-19; 64: 18a).

Lord, do your eyes not see the truth? If our iniquities testify against us, act for your name, O Lord, for our iniquities are various. We have sinned against you; You who is the hope of Israel, his savior in time of distress, why should you be as a stranger in the land, like a traveler who enters to spend the night? Why should you be as incompetent hero who can save us? You are however among us, O Lord, and your name is called on us. Do not abandon us! We hope for peace, and nothing happy happens, a time of healing, and behold trouble! Lord, we recognize our wickedness, the iniquity of our fathers, for we have sinned against you. Because of your name do not despise, do not disgrace the throne of your glory! Remember, do not break your alliance with us! Is it not you, Lord our God? We hope in you, for you have made all these things (Jeremiah 5: 3a; 14: 7-9; 19b-21, 22b).

Lord, my strength and my support, and my refuge in the day of trouble! Heal me LORD, and I shall be healed, save me, and shall be saved. For you are my praise, do not make me a subject of fright, you, my refuge in time of trouble! (Jeremiah 16: 19a; 17: 14, 17).

Lord, GOD, big and redoubtable God, you who keeps your alliance and mercy for those who love you and keep your commandments. We have sinned, we have committed iniquity, we have done wickedly and have rebelled, we have turned away from your commandments and from your judgments.

To you, Lord, the Justice, but to us, confusion of face. Yes Lord, to us confusion of face, because we have sinned against you. To the Lord our God, mercy, and forgiveness! And now, O Lord our God, you who brought your people out of Egypt by the strong hand, and hast gotten thee renown, as at this day. We have sinned, we have committed the iniquity, O Lord. According to righteousness, let your anger and your fury be turned away from us, for because of our sins and the iniquities of our fathers, your people are in reproach to all who are around us. And now, O our God, hear the prayer and supplication of your servant.

My God, incline your ear and hear. Open your eyes and see our desolations, and the city upon which your name is called! For it is not because of our righteousness that we present you our supplications.

It is because of your great mercy, Lord, hear! Lord, forgive! Lord, listen! Act and soon, for your sake, O my God! For your name is called upon your city and your people (Daniel 9: 4b-5, 7a, 8a, 8c, 9a, 16-16a, 16c-17a, 18-19).

Are you not from the everlasting, O LORD my God, my holy? We will not die! O LORD, you have created this people for judgment O my God. You have created punishment. Ah! Lord, let you ear be attentive to the prayer of your servant and to the prayer of your servants who want to fear your name! In anger, remember your mercy! (Habakuk1: 12; Nehemiah 1: 11a; Habakkuk 3: 2d), Lord, save me! Have mercy on me, Lord, Son of David! (Matthew 14: 30; 15: 22a)

Increase our faith! I believe! Help me for my unbelief! Father, if you were willing to remove this cup from me! However, may my willing not done, but yours!
(Luke 17: 5; Mark 9: 24b; Luke 22: 42).

4. Prayer for the New Year and Birthday

Before the mountains were brought forth, and that you had made the earth and the world, from everlasting to everlasting you are God. You let the men get in the dust and you say, son of man, go back! For a thousand years are in your sight as the day of yesterday, when it is no more, and as a watch of the night. You take them away like a dream that in the morning brands like the grass:

It blooms in the morning and it goes, the cut it in the evening, and it withers. We are consumed by your anger and wrath terrifies us. You put our iniquities at your front, and in the light of your face, our secret sins. All our days pass away under your wrath; we see our years vanishing as a tale that sounds.

The days of our years are seventy years, for the lasting it is eighty years and the pride they take in is only pain and sorrow, for they quickly pass, and we disappear. Who is frightened of the power of your anger and your wrath. According, to the fear that is due to you, teach us to know our days, so that we may apply our heart to wisdom? Come back, Lord! Until when? Have compassion on your servants! O satisfy us every morning with your mercy and we will be all our life with joy and gladness. Let your work appear on your servants, and your glory unto their children! Psalm 90: 2-14, 16).

Who am I, O, Everlasting Lord, and what is my house so that you may have sent me where I am? I am too small for all grace and faithfulness's which you have sewed to your servant. I will not let you go before you had blessed me.

I hope for your salvation, O, LORD (2 Samuel 7: 18b; Genesis 32: 10a, 49: 18) you have given me your grace with life; you have kept me under your care and under your grace. Think positively upon me, O my God! Your word is a lamp to my feet and a light for my path. Strengthen my steps in thy word and don't let any iniquity have power over me! Let your face shine on your servant and teach me your commandments! (Job 10 a; 49: 18). You've given me your grace with life, you've kept me under your care and your grace. Think upon me, O my God! Think positively upon me, O my God! Your word is a lamp to my feet and a light for my path. Strengthen my steps in your word and don't let any iniquity have power over me! Let your face shine on your servant and teach me your commandments!

You've given me your grace with life, you've kept me under your care and your grace. Think upon me, O my God! Your word is a lamp to my feet and a light for my path! (Job 10: 12; Nehemiah 13: 31b; Psalm 119: 10, 133, 135).

Lord! You prospect me and you know me, you know when I sit and when I stand, you know from far away my thought, you know when I walk and when I lie down, and you are on all my ways. For the word is not my tongue, that O Lord! You know it altogether. You have beset me behind and before, and lay your hand upon me. So, a wonderful Knowledge is beyond me; it is too high for me to reach it. Where far shall I go from your spirit, and where far can I flee from your presence? If I am in the heavens, you are there, if I am buried you are there. If I take the wings of the morning and dwell in the extremity of the sea, even there too your hand will guide me, your right hand will follow me. If I say, the darkness shall cover me at night, you shall become light around me, even the darkness is not dark to the light, and I praise you for I am wonderful creature. Your work is admirable and my soul recognizes well.

When I was a shapeless mass, your eyes saw me and in your book, were registered the days planned for me, before one of them existed. Your thoughts, O God, seem inscrutable to me! That number is great! If I count them, they will be more than the grains of sand. Observe me, O God, and know my heart. Test me and know my thoughts! See if I'm on the wrong path and lead my thoughts! See if I'm on the wrong path and lead me in the everlasting way! (Psalm 139: 1-12, 14, 16-18a, 23-24).

5. Prayer in distress or illness

When I call, answer me God of my righteousness! When I am in trouble, save me! Have mercy on me, hear my prayer! As the deer pants for the water brooks, so my soul pants for you, O God! My soul is cast down within me. Deep calls another deep at the roar of your waterfalls; all your waves and your billows are gone over me (Psalm 4: 2; 42: 2.7A, 8).

Before I was afflicted I was losing myself; now I keep your word. It is good for me to be humiliated, that I might learn your commandments, I know, O LORD that your judgments are right, it is in faithfulness you have afflicted me. May your kindness be for my comfort, as you have promised to your servant! Let your tender mercies come unto me, that I may live! My eyes languishing for your promise, I say "when will you comfort me? If the law had not made my delight, I should then have perished in my affliction. Support me according to your promise, so that I may live, and let me not be ashamed of my hope! Be my support, that I may be saved and that I deal constantly with your commandments! Turn your face to me and have mercy on me according to your habit towards those who like your name! Consider my affliction and deliver me! For I do not forget your law" (Psalm 119: 67, 71, 77a; 82; 116; 117; 132; 153)

You have forgotten men for long, Lord forever? How long will you hide me your face? How long shall I take counsel in my soul and every day sorrow in my heart? Look, answer me, O Lord my God, gives clarity to my eyes, so that I may not fall asleep as the death of sleep. I have confidence in your goodness, I have joy in the heart, because of your salvation (Psalm 13: 2,3a, 4.6a).

My God! My God! Why have you forsaken me and delay to help me, my groaning? My God, I cry by day, and you do not answer; in night and I have no rest. However, you are the holy, you sit in the praises of Israel. Our fathers trusted you; they trusted and you delivered them. They cried to you and were saved; he trusted in you and they were not ashamed. Be not far from me, for trouble is near and there is none to help me! And you, O LORD, be not far! You who is my strength, may you come quickly to help me (Psalm 22: 2 to 6.15, 20).

Lord! I seek my refuge in you, I would never be ashamed, deliver me in your right! Turn your ear to me, may you not hesitate to help me! Be my rock of refuge, a fortress where I find my salvation! For you are my rock, my fortress, and because of your name you guide me, you guide me. For you are my protector. I commend my spirit into your hands, you have redeemed me, O LORD God of truth! I'll be by your grace glad and rejoice; because you see my misery, you know the anguish of my soul. You set my feet off, the soul and the body worn out by grief. My life is spent with sorrow and my years with sighing. My strength fails because of my iniquity, and my bones are consumed. All my opponents have made me an object of opprobrium, of great shame for neighbors and a fear to my friends. I am like a broken vessel. But I trust in you, O Lord I say you are my God! My times are in your hand.

Let your face shine on your servant, save me by your grace! Lord! I am not mistaken when I cry. Oh! How great is your goodness that you have reserved for those who fear you that you show to those who seek refuge in you, in sight of the son of man! Your protectors under the shelter of the face against those who persecute you in your tent's guards against the strife of tongues. I said in my haste, I am cast out of your sight but you hear the voice of my supplications when I cried unto you (Psalm 31: 6 2-3,5a, 8,9b-12a, 13b, 15-16a, 17-18a, 20 to 21.23).

Lord! Tell me what is my end? What is the measure of my days; that I may know how frail I am. Behold, you have made my days as the width of the hand and my life is as nothing before you. Indeed! Every man standing is nothing but vanity. Now, Lord, what can I expect? My hope is in you.

Hear my prayer, O Lord, and give ear unto my cry; do not be silent at my tears! For I am a host by you, a resident as all my fathers (Psalm 39: 5-6, 8.13). You Lord! You won't refuse my mercies; your kindness and faithfulness will continually preserve me. For various evils have surrounded me; the punishment of my iniquities reach me and I cannot stand their sight. They are more than the hair of my head and my courage gives up. May you deliver me, O Lord, Lord, come quickly to my aid! Let all those who seek you be glad and rejoice in you! Let those who love your salvation say continually: Exalted be the Lord! (Psalm 40: 12, 14, 17).

You hold my eyelids awake and in my confusion, I cannot speak. I will tell your works to LORD, for I will remember your wonders of past times; I will speak to you of all works, I will declare the great acts. O GOD! Your ways are holy. Which GOD is as big as God? You are the God who does wonders; you showed your power among the peoples. Remember what period of my life is (Psalm 77: 5.12 to 15, 89: 48a).

Lord, hear my prayer and let my cry come till you. Do not hide your face from me in the day of my distress! Incline your ear to me when I call! Don't hesitate to raise me! My days are like a shadow at its decimation and I am withered like grass. But you, Lord! You reign forever and your memory lasts for generations. I said, my God, don't take me away in the midst of my days, you, whose years last forever!

You have first founded the earth, and the heavens are the work of your hands. They shall perish, but you shall endure. They all wear out like a garment; you will change them like clothing and they will be changed. But you are the same, and the years have no end. (Psalms 102: 2-3, 12-13, 25-28).

Lord, they sought you, when they were in trouble; they spread in prayer, when you punished them. O Lord! I am distressed, help me! Lord, look at my distress! For my sighs are many, and my heart is faint. Chastise me, O LORD But with equity and not in your anger, fearing to bringing me to nothing. You are too right, O LORD, when I plead with you (Isaiah 26: 16; 38: 14c; Lamentations 1: 20a, 22c; Jeremiah 10: 24; 12: 1a).

When I walk in the shadow of the valley of death, I will fear no evil, for you are with me; your rod and your staff comfort me.

CHAPTER 18

GUIDE TO READ THE BIBLE IN ONE YEAR

JANUARY		FEBRUARY	
DATE	**REFERENCES**	**DATE**	**REFERENCES**
1st	John 1 : 1-18	1st	Job 21-22
02	Psalm 1-3 ; Proverbs 10: 1-6	02	Job 23
		03	Job 24-25
03	Genesis 1-2	04	Job 26-27
04	Genesis 3-4	05	Job 28
05	Genesis	06	Psalm 12-14;Proverbs 11:1-6
06	Genesis 6-7		
07	Genesis 8-9	07	Job 29-30
08	Genesis 10	08	Job 31-32
09	Psalm 4-5 ; Proverbs 10: 7-12	09	Job 33
		10	Job 34-35
10	Genesis 11-12	11	Job 36-37
11	Genesis 13-14	12	Job 38
12	Genesis 15	13	Psalm 15-17, Proverbs.11:7-12
13	Genesis 16-17		
14	Genesis 18-19	14	Job 39-40
15	Genesis 20	15	Job 41-42
16	Psalms 6-7 ; Proverbs 10: 13-18	16	Genesis 23
		17	Genesis 24-25
17	Genesis 21-22	18	Genesis 26-27
18	Job 1-2	19	Genesis 28
19	Job 3	20	Psalm 18:1-25; Proverbs 11
20	Job 4-5	21	13-18
21	Job 6-7		Genesis 29-30
22	Job 8	22	Genesis 31-32
23	Psalms 8-9; Proverbs 10: 19-25	23	Genesis 33
		24	Genesis 34-35
24	Job 9-10	25	Genesis 36
25	Job 11-12	26	Genesis 37
26	Job 13	27	Genesis 38
27	Job 14-15	28	Psalm 18:26-51; Proverbs 11:19-25
28	Job 16-17		
29	Job 18	29	Genesis 39-40
30	Psalm 10-11; Proverbs 10:26-32		
31	Job 19-20		

MARCH		APRIL	
DATE	**REFERENCES**	**DATE**	**REFERENCES**
1st	Genesis 41-42	1st	Exodus 36-37
02	Genesis 43	02	Exodus 38
03	Genesis 44-45	03	Psalm 25-26;Proverbs
04	Genesis 46-47		12:19-24
05	Genesis 48	04	Exodus 39-40
06	Psalm 19; Proverbs 11: 26-	05	Leviticus 1-2
	31	06	Leviticus 3
07	Genesis 49-50	07	Leviticus 4-5
08	Exodus 1-2	08	Leviticus 6-7
09	Exodus 3	09	Leviticus 8
10	Exodus 4-5	10	Psalm 27-29;
11	Exodus 6-7	11	Proverbs 12:25-28
12	Exodus 8	12	Leviticus 9-10
13	Psalm 20-21, Proverbs 12:	13	Leviticus 11-12
	1-6	14	Leviticus 13
14	Exodus 9-10	15	Leviticus 14-15
15	Exodus 11-12	16	Leviticus 16-17
16	Exodus 13	17	Leviticus 18
17	Exodus 14-15	18	Psalm 30; Proverbs
18	Exodus 16-17		13 :1-6
19	Exodus 18	19	Leviticus 19-20
20	Psalm 22 ; Proverbs 12 :7-	20	Leviticus 21-22
	12	21	Leviticus 23
21	Exodus 19-20	22	Leviticus 24-25
22	Exodus 21-22	23	Leviticus 26-27
23	Exodus 23	24	Numbers 1
24	Exodus 24-25	25	Proverbs 13: 7-12
25	Exodus 26-27	26	Numbers 2-3
26	Exodus 28	27	Numbers 4-5
27	Psalm 23; Proverbs 12: 13-	28	Numbers 6
	18	29	Numbers 7-8
28	Exodus 29-30	30	Numbers 9-10
29	Exodus 31-32	31	Numbers 11
30	Exodus 33		
31	Exodus 34-35		

MAY		JUNE	
DATE	**REFERENCES**	**DATE**	**REFERENCES**
1st	Psalms 32-33; Proverbs 13:13-18	1st	Deuteronomy 19-20
02	Numbers 12-13	02	Deuteronomy 21-22
03	Numbers 14-15	03	Deuteronomy 23
04	Numbers 16	04	Deuteronomy 24-25
05	Numbers 17-18	05	Psalm 37:21-40;Proverbs 14:21-27
06	Numbers 19-20	06	Deuteronomy 26-27
07	Numbers 21	07	Deuteronomy 28
08	Psalm 34; Proverbs 13: 19-25	08	Deuteronomy 29
09	Numbers 22-23	09	Deutéronome 31
10	Numbers 24-25	10	Deuteronomy 32-33
11	Numbers 26	11	Deuteronomy 34
12	Numbers 27-28	12	Psalm 38; Proverbs 14:28-33
13	Numbers 29-30	13	Joshua 1-2
14	Numbers 31	14	Joshua 3-4
15	Psalm 35; Proverbs 14:1-6	15	Joshua 5
16	Numbers 32-33	16	Joshua 6-7
17	Numbers 34	17	Joshua 8-9
18	Numbers 35-36	18	Joshua 10
19	Deuteronomy 1-2	19	Psalm 39-40; Proverbs 15:15-6
20	Deuteronomy 3	20	Joshua 11-12
21	Deuteronomy 4-5	21	Joshua 13-14
22	Psalm 36; Proverbs 14: 7-13	22	Joshua 15
23	Deuteronomy 6-7	23	Joshua 16-17
24	Deuteronomy 8	24	Joshua 18-19
25	Deuteronomy 9-10	25	Joshua 20
26	Deuteronomy 11-12	26	Psalm 41-43; Proverbs 15:7-13
27	Deuteronomy 13	27	Joshua 21-22
28	Deuteronomy 14-15	28	Joshua 23
29	Psalm 37:1-20; Proverbs 14:14-20	29	Joshua 24
30	Deuteronomy 16-17	30	Judges 1-2
31	Deuteronomy 18		

JULY		AUGUST	
DATE	**REFERENCES**	**DATE**	**REFERENCES**
1st	Judges 3-4	1st	1 Samuel 21
02	Judges 5	02	1 Samuel 22-23
03	Psalm 44; Proverbs15:14-20	03	1 Samuel 24-25
04	Judges 6-7	04	1 Samuel 26
05	Judges 8-9	05	1 Samuel 27-28
06	Judges 10	06	1 Samuel 29-30
07	Judges 11-12	07	Psalm 51; Proverbs
08	Judges 13-14		16:14-20
09	Judges 15	08	1 Samuel 31
10	Psalm45-46; Proverbs	09	2 Samuel 1-2
	15:21-27	10	2 Samuel 3-4
11	Judges 16-17	11	2 Samuel 5
12	Judges 18-19	12	2 Samuel 6-7
13	Judges 20	13	2 Samuel 8-9
14	Judges 21	14	Psalm 52-53; Proverbs
15	Ruth 1-2		16: 21-27
16	Ruth 3-4	15	2 Samuel 10
17	Psalm 47-48; Proverbs 15:	16	2 Samuel 11-12
18	28-33	17	2 Samuel 13-14
	1 Samuel 1	18	2 Samuel 15
19	1 Samuel 2-3	19	2 Samuel 16-17
20	1 Samuel 4-5	20	2 Samuel 18-19
21	1 Samuel 6	21	Psalm 54-55; Proverbs
22	1 Samuel 7-8		16:28-33
23	1 Samuel 9-10	22	2 Samuel 20
24	Psalm 49; Proverbs 16 : 1-6	23	2 Samuel 21-22
25	1 Samuel 11	24	2 Samuel 23-24
26	1 Samuel 12-13	25	1 Rois 1
27	1 Samuel 14-15	26	1 Rois 2-3
28	1 Samuel 16	27	1 Rois 4
29	1 Samuel 17-18	28	1 Psalm 56-57; Proverbs
30	1 Samuel 19-20		17: 1-6
31	Psalm 50; Proverbs 167-13	29	Proverbs 1-2
		30	Proverbs 3-4
		31	Proverbs 5

SEPTEMBER		OCTOBER	
DATE	**REFERENCES**	**DATE**	**REFERENCES**
1st	Proverbs 6-7	1st	1 Kings 20-21
02	Proverbs 8-9	02	1 Kings 22
03	Songs 8-9	03	2 Kings 1-2
04	Psalm 58-59 ; Proverbs17: 7-12	04	2 Kings 3-4
05	Songs 2-3	05	Psalm 66-67;Proverbs 18: 7-12
06	Songs 4-5	06	2 Kings 5
07	Songs 6	07	2 Kings 6-7
08	Songs 7-8	08	2 Kings 8-9
09	1 Kings 5-6	09	2 Kings 10
10	1 Kings 7-8	10	2 Kings 11-12
11	Psalm 60-61; Proverbs 17: 13-17	11	2 Kings 13
12	1 Kings 9	12	Psalm 68; Proverbs 18: 13-17
13	1 Kings 10-11	13	2 Kings 14 : 1-25
14	Eclesiastes 1-2	14	Jonas 1-2
15	Eclesiastes 3	15	Jonas 3-4
16	Eclesiastes 4-5	16	2 Kings 14 : 26-29
17	Eclesiastes 6-7	17	Amos 1-2
18	Psalm 62-63; Proverbs 17:18-24	18	Amos 3-4
19	Eclesiastes 8	19	Psalm 69; Proverbs 18: 18-24
20	Eclesiastes 9-10	20	Amos 5
21	Eclesiastes 11-12	21	Amos 6-7
22	1 Kings 12	22	Amos 8-9
23	Eclesiastes 9-10	23	2 Kings 15
24	Eclesiastes 11-12	24	2 Kings 16-17
25	1 Kings 12	25	2 Kings 18-19
26	1 Kings 13-14	26	Psalm 70-71; Proverbs 19: 1-6
27	1 Kings 15-16	27	2 Kings 20
28	Psalm 64-65; Proverbs 18: 1-6	28	2 Kings 20
29	1 Kings 17	29	2 Kings 21-22
30	1 Kings 18-19	30	2 Kings 23-24

NOVEMBER		DECEMBER	
DATE	REFERENCES	DATE	REFERENCES
1st	2 Kings 25	1st	Joël 3-4
02	1 Chronicles 1-5	02	Obadiah
03	1 Chronicles 6-9	03	2 Chronicles 23-24
04	Psalm 72 ; Proverbs 19: 7-12	04	Psalm 78: 1-35;
		05	Proverbs 20 :7-12
05	1 Chronicles 10	06	2 Chronicles 25-26 : 8
06	1 Chronicles 11-12	07	Isaiah 1-2
07	1 Chronicles 13-14	08	Isaiah 3
08	1 Chronicles 15	09	Isaiah 4-5
09	1 Chronicles 16-17	10	Isaiah 6
10	1 Chronicles 18-19	11	2 Chronicles 26:9- 23
11	Psalm73; Proverbs 19: 13-17	12	Psalm 78 : 36-72
		13	Proverbs 20: 13-18
12	1 Chronicles 20	14	2 Chronicles s 27-28
13	1 Chronicles 21-22	15	2 Chronicles 29-30
14	1 Chronicles 23-24	16	2 Chronicles 31
15	1 Chronicles 25	17	2 Chronicles 32
16	1 Chronicles 26-27	18	Isaiah 7-8
17	1 Chronicles 28-29	19	Isaiah 9-10
18	Psalm 74;Proverbs 19: 18-23	20	Psalm 79 ; Proverbs 20: 19-23
19	2 Chronicles 1-5	21	Isaiah 11
20	2 Chronicles 6-8	22	Isaiah 12-13
21	2 Chronicles 9-10	23	Isaiah 14-15
	Psalm75-	24	Isaiah 16
22	76;Proverbs19:24-29	25	Isaiah 17-18
23	2 Chronicles 11	26	Isaiah 19-20
24	2 Chronicles 12-13	27	Psalm 80; Proverbs 20: 24-30
25	2 Chronicles 14-15		
26	2 Chronicles 16	28	Isaiah 21-22
27	2 Chronicles 17-18	29	Isaiah 23-24
28	2 Chronicles 19-20	30	Isaiah 25-26
29	Psalm 77 ; Proverbs 20: 1-6	31	Isaiah 27-28 Isaiah 29-30
30	2 Chronicles 21-22		

CHAPTER 19

131 GREAT PRAYERS

1) I bind all spirits acting against the answer to my prayers in the Name of Jesus Christ of Nazareth.

2) I disarm any power that have made alliance with soil, water, and wind about me in the name of Jesus Christ of Nazareth.

3) I release myself from every donation of blood to the wizard in the Name of Jesus Christ of Nazareth.

4) I release myself of any food or drink taken at satanic table in my sleep in the name of Jesus Christ of Nazareth.

5) Let my oppressors fight against each other in the name of Jesus Christ of Nazareth.

6) O Lord, begin to baptize every part of my life with your powerful miracles in the name of Jesus Christ of Nazareth

7) I ordered the forces drinking milk of my life to start now throwing it in the name of Jesus Christ of Nazareth.

8) That all decisions made by the wizards against me be null and void in the name of Jesus Christ of Nazareth.

9) O Lord slap the face of every word that rises against me and broke the jaw of evil in the name of Jesus Christ of Nazareth.

10) Every evil mirror of control used against me under water be completely broken into pieces in the name of Jesus Christ Nazareth.

11) That GOD whirlwind scatters every satanic meeting about me in the name of Jesus Christ of Nazareth.

12) O Lord, transform me into hot coal in front of the wicked.

13) Lord opens doors of opportunities for me through these prayers.

14) Tree of poverty in my life, I order you to dry in name of Jesus Christ of Nazareth.

15) Walls physical and spiritual opposition, I order you to fall like ripe Jericho in the name of Jesus Christ of Nazareth.

16) May only new fountains appear in my desert in the name of Jesus Christ of Nazareth.

17) I order every crooked and difficult parts of my life to start providing testimonies in the name of Jesus Christ of Nazareth.

18) O Lord turn my mourning in life and my tears into joy in the name of Jesus Christ of Nazareth.

19) May all those that sit on the way to my prosperity and who swore that I would not blow start by making the barrel several times in the name of Jesus Christ of Nazareth.

20) My lord use the white and black to bless me in the name of Jesus Christ of Nazareth.

21) May the sun of my prosperity rise and scatter any cloud of the poverty of my life in the name of Jesus Christ of Nazareth.

22) I withdraw my blessings of water, forest and satanic banks in the name of Jesus Christ of Nazareth.

23) That the goods of the disbelievers may be transferred into my hands in the name of Jesus Christ of Nazareth.

24) My lord make me a reference center of supernatural blessings in the name of Jesus Christ of Nazareth.

25) Plunge me in the river of prosperity in the name of Jesus Christ of Nazareth

26) May any identifying mark of witchcraft in my life be taken away at once in the name of Jesus Christ of Nazareth.

27) May tall my stubborn pursuers be as stubble by the wind in the name of Jesus Christ of Nazareth.

28) That the fire of prayer pursues and destroys all the mighty men of my life in the name of Jesus Christ of Nazareth

29) May all winds and satanic storms be silenced in the name of Jesus Christ of Nazareth.

30) That all my disappointments become appointment in the name of Jesus Christ of Nazareth.

31) May all my years and my lost efforts be converted into multiplied blessings in the name of Jesus Christ of Nazareth

32) O Lord, make in my life a miracle that will astonish the world in the name of Jesus Christ of Nazareth.

33) I take away my stolen opening keys that the enemy has stolen in the name of Jesus Christ of Nazareth.

34) May all satanic snake sent against my destiny receives the opposition and be sent back to the sender in the name of Jesus Christ of Nazareth.

35) That any debt fortress in my life tumbles this month in the name of Jesus Christ of Nazareth.

36) I order to the rain of happiness abundance to fall in the departments of my life in the name of Jesus Christ of Nazareth

37) I withdraw my name from the book of all premature death in the name of Jesus Christ of Nazareth.

38) I refuse any work without profit in the name of Jesus Christ of Nazareth.

39) I order that my image used in the satanic kingdom to control my life, my finances and my family be consumed till ashes in the name of Jesus Christ of Nazareth.

40) I stand in the blood of Jesus Christ and I proclaim victory over Satan and his angels in the name of Jesus Christ of Nazareth.

41) I spread the blood of Jesus Christ on my body from the top of the head to the feet in the name of Jesus Christ of Nazareth.

42) By the blood of Jesus Christ I fight against any evil design led against my life in the name of Jesus Christ of Nazareth.

43) May all doors opened by Satan, demons or witches in my life be forever closed by the blood of Jesus Christ in the name of Jesus Christ of Nazareth.

44) May all diseases circulating in my blood to be evacuated by the blood of Jesus Christ in the name of Jesus Christ of Nazareth.

45) May all food eaten at the table of demons be purified in my stomach by the blood of Jesus Christ in the name of Jesus Christ of Nazareth.

46) I order any diseases circulating in my body to die in the name of Jesus Christ of Nazareth.

47) I reduce to nil any spirit of death that lurks around me and I cancel all appointments with him in the name of Jesus Christ of Nazareth

48) May any dead body organ in my life receive life in the name of Jesus Christ of Nazareth.

49) May any incantation pronounced against me be canceled in the name of Jesus Christ of Nazareth.

50) I stop any off and landing of witches against me in the name of Jesus Christ of Nazareth.

51) May GOD's whirlwind scatter all night meeting about me in the name of Jesus Christ of Nazareth.

52) An evil alliance that attacks my destiny, I disconnect you from my life in the name of Jesus Christ of Nazareth.

53) May any damage created in my life through alliances be repaired by the fire of the Holy Spirit in the name of Jesus Christ of Nazareth.

54) May the Satanic blood links existing in my family and that affect it and my life be broken in the name of Jesus Christ of Nazareth.

55) O God arise and use all the weapons at your disposal to humiliate my enemies in the name of Jesus Christ of Nazareth.

56) May all powers giving rise to affliction in my life through dreams be buried alive in the name of Jesus Christ of Nazareth.

57) Let every word that I have pronounced in convents by fetishists be canceled by the blood of Jesus Christ in the name of Jesus Christ of Nazareth.

58) I make void and helpless and powerless all animal sacrifice made about me and I return I send back the spell to the priest in the name of Jesus Christ of Nazareth.

59) May all corporation of wizards and witches against my life, be dismantled in the name of Jesus Christ of Nazareth.

60) The Fire of the Holy Spirit may burn my name from the book of premature death in the name of Jesus Christ of Nazareth.

61) That all diabolical sacrifice made against me in an intersection be canceled by the blood of Jesus Christ in the name of Jesus Christ of Nazareth.

62) May all evil padlocks used as bank for my blessing be broken through the fire hammer in the name of Jesus Christ of Nazareth.

63) May all eyes watching my thought receive fiery arrow in the Name of Jesus Christ of Nazareth.

64) All those who make public my name for evil be publicly humiliated in the name of Jesus Christ of Nazareth.

65) Lord, broaden supernaturally my sides in the name of Jesus Christ of Nazareth.

66) Let my prayers liberate the intervention of angels in my favor in the name of Jesus Christ of Nazareth.

67) You, root of all hereditary diseases which ravage my paternal or maternal family that the fire of the Holy Spirit burns you in the name of Jesus Christ of Nazareth.

68) Lord, give me a new start with a spring that will allow me to catch up all the lost years in the name of Jesus Christ of Nazareth.

69) I reject the names that change my destiny in the name of Jesus Christ of Nazareth.

70) May all arrows, shots, injury, harassment of opposition in dreams, be returned to the sender in the name of Jesus Christ of Nazareth.

71) I destroy every evil spirit that works through my name since my birth in the name of Jesus Christ of Nazareth.

72) May the Blood of Jesus Christ erase any adverse effects in my life basing on my name, in the name of Jesus Christ of Nazareth.

73) Holy Spirit of God, open my eyes so that I can see and my ears so that I can hear all curses hidden in the name of Jesus Christ of Nazareth.

74) Lord, clear me from any signs and any orders that condemn me because of my name in the name of Jesus Christ of Nazareth.

75) That all forces of darkness that want to handle my name be rebuked in the name of Jesus Christ of Nazareth.

76) Any fatal useless name given to me by a parent or grandparent for reincarnation or to commemorate an event is canceled by the blood of Jesus Christ and in the name of Jesus Christ of Nazareth.

77) I claim all the blessings that are attached to my name in the name of Jesus Christ of Nazareth.

78) I convert and multiply whenever I said yes to an evil name with the blessing, the success and elevation in the name of Jesus Christ of Nazareth.

79) You who said: Abraham, I will make your name great, Make my great name for the rest of my life.

80) May the wind of the resurrection uproot all the bad ancestral or parental foundations that affect any part of my life in the name of Jesus Christ of Nazareth.

81) I order any spirit of division to move away from my married life in the name of Jesus Christ of Nazareth.

82) I confess all known sin or any sin not bound to my name (given by my parents) in the name of Jesus Christ of Nazareth.

83) That all the forces of darkness that want to handle my name be reprimanded by the fire of the Holy Spirit in the name of Jesus Christ of Nazareth.

84) I destroy every evil spirit that will call my name somewhere to destroy or to manipulate the name of Jesus Christ of Nazareth.

85) All thrones of witchcraft in my household must be located and dismantled by GOD's thunder in the name of Jesus Christ of Nazareth

86) That all coffin fashioned against me by a sorcerer returns against to the author himself in the name of Jesus Christ of Nazareth.

87) (Points to the sky) I talk to the sun, moon, and stars to shine in my favor in the name of Jesus Christ of Nazareth.

88) (Pointe finger earth) anything planned against me in the earth is broken up by the fire of God in the name of Jesus Christ of Nazareth.

89) That all spirit of water mermaid with a mission to destroy my home must destroyed by the fire of the Holy Spirit in the name of Jesus Christ of Nazareth.

90) That all agreement I consciously or unconsciously signed with the mermaid is broken by the Blood of Jesus Christ and in the name of Jesus Christ of Nazareth.

91) Whether any object or organ of my body that I have given for a consultation and representing me in the kingdom of the spirit of the water mermaid is burned by the fire of God and in the name of Jesus Christ of Nazareth.

92) May the fire of God release me from all spiritual husband and wife in the name of Jesus Christ of Nazareth.

93) May all that the mermaid has made in my life be uprooted and consumed by the fire of the Holy Spirit in the name of Jesus Christ of Nazareth

94) May signs of water mermaid in my life that keep me from getting married be cleared by the Blood of Jesus Christ in the name of Jesus Christ of Nazareth.

95) May signs of water mermaid in my life that keep me from being fruitful be cleared by the blood of Jesus Christ in the name of Jesus Christ of Nazareth.

96) May signs of water mermaid in my life that cause problems in my home be cleared by the blood of Jesus Christ in the name of Jesus Christ of Nazareth.

97) May all siren agent that considers itself like my friend, my companion, to destroy my life be put out of harm's way;

98) May all shell placed over my eyes by the siren to make me believe that I am happy to be taken away by the blood of Jesus Christ in the name of Jesus Christ of Nazareth.

99) May all my natural property confiscated by the siren buried in the sea or land be vomited and returned in the name of Jesus Christ Nazareth.

100) May any label on my body put by the spirit of water siren to recognize me, be cleared by the blood of Jesus Christ in the name of Jesus Christ of Nazareth

101) May all my antagonists be cloistered in shame and confusion in the name of Jesus Christ of Nazareth.

102) May the dress photo wedding ring or any equipment used for my wedding in the spiritual world be burned by the fire of thunder GOD!

103) May any marriage certificate that keeps me in the circle of water mermaid be burned by the fire of the Holy Spirit in the name of Jesus Christ of Nazareth.

104) May the head of the snake lodged in my life that allows a husband or wife at night to control my life be broken by fire hammer in the name of Jesus Christ of Nazareth!

105) I renounce and reject the name given to me by the husband or wife of the night in the spiritual world in the name of Jesus Christ of Nazareth.

106) That a trademark in my life and on my forehead with the satanic marriage be erased forever from my life in the name of Jesus Christ of Nazareth.

107) Every satanic writing or any letter written by the husband or wife of the night about me be canceled.

108) That all demoniac evil on my face that keeps me from meeting my soul mate or my side for the marriage to be teared.

109) That all children I had in the spiritual world that

prevent me from conceiving fall and die so that I conceive in the name of Jesus Christ of Nazareth.

110) That a power that oppresses my marriage falls and dies in the name of Jesus Christ of Nazareth.

111) I ask for divorce and I give up my marriage with the husband or wife of the night in the name of Jesus Christ of Nazareth.

112) I withdraw my blood, my uterus or any other part of my body stolen by husband and wife of the night in the name of Jesus Christ of Nazareth.

113) Lord repairs and restores any part of my body destroyed by the husband and wife the night of the name of Jesus Christ of Nazareth.

114) May any coalition of women or night or night husband against me be troubled in the name of Jesus Christ of Nazareth!

115) I pronounce the divorce between me and you (wife or husband at night) in the name of Jesus Christ of Nazareth.

116) May a threat following the divorce against you return to sender in the name of Jesus Christ of Nazareth.

117) That the hell greatly opens his mouth and swallows all people who suck my happiness and my life in the name of Jesus Christ of Nazareth.

118) Let my name be a torch, a boiling volcano to all who will call to follow me or hurt me in the name of Jesus Christ of Nazareth.

119) All the Herods of my life receiving the blows of angels and to be corroded by the name of Jesus Christ of Nazareth!

120) Lord, causes an explosion of power around me in order to destroy anything that does not come from you about my life in the name of Jesus Christ of Nazareth.

121) Lord, makes my enemies 7 times the harm they did to me in the name of Jesus Christ of Nazareth.

122) Lord Makes all those who seek life as dung for the earth in the name of Jesus Christ of Nazareth.

123) Lord moves the kidneys of all perpetrators of anti-drilled posts, anti-peace, anti-marriage in the name of Jesus Christ of Nazareth.

124) All those who pursue me day and night, Lord finds them a home in the bush in the name of Jesus Christ of Nazareth.

125) Set me up so I walk on my enemies and their works in the name of Jesus Christ of Nazareth.

126) I break any mirror monitor and spiritual erected against me in the name of Jesus Christ of Nazareth.

127) Lord, transform me in burning coal against my enemies in the name of Jesus Christ of Nazareth.

128) May all the mockery of my opponents be converted into honor in the name of Jesus Christ of Nazareth.

129) May all written negative thing in the cycle of the moon against my destiny be cleared by the blood of Jesus Christ in the name of Jesus Christ of Nazareth.

130) Lose your control on my life and be forever driven out of my life (diabolical incision, satanic dream, consecration evil, satanic sacrifice, curse of parents, demoniac blood, devilish change destiny, diabolical hands of tax) in the name of Jesus Christ of Nazareth.

131) I dive all my inquiries in the blood of Jesus Christ in the name of Jesus Christ of Nazareth.

AMEN!

**To correspond with Elvis Dagba,
you may write to him :**

P. O. BOX 9733
Norfolk, VA 23505

Tel : (757) 453-4969

Email : elvisdagba@elvisdagba.org

Website : elvisdagba.org

www.ingramcontent.com/pod-product-compliance
Lightning Source LLC
LaVergne TN
LVHW021401080426
835508LV00020B/2393

* 9 7 8 0 9 9 8 4 4 2 8 0 8 *